MEN EXPLAIN THINGS TO ME

Men
Explain
Things
to Me

REBECCA SOLNIT

Images by Ana Teresa Fernandez

 Haymarket Books
Chicago, Illinois

 Dispatch Books

© 2014 Rebecca Solnit

Haymarket Books
PO Box 180165
Chicago, IL 60618
773-583-7884
info@haymarketbooks.org
www.haymarketbooks.org

ISBN: 978-1-60846-496-8

Trade distribution:
In the US, through Consortium Book Sales and Distribution, www.cbsd.com
In Canada, Publishers Group Canada, www.pgcbooks.ca

Special discounts are available for bulk purchases by organizations and institutions.
Please contact Haymarket Books for more information at 773-583-7884
or info@haymarketbooks.org.

This book was published with the generous support of Lannan Foundation and the
Wallace Action Fund.

Cover design by Abby Weintraub. Interior images © Ana Teresa Fernandez.

Library of Congress Cataloging-in-Publication Data is available.

Printed in Canada by union labor.

10 9 8 7 6 5 4 3

RECYCLED
Paper made from
recycled material
FSC® C103567

For the grandmothers, the levelers, the dreamers, the men who get it,

the young women who keep going, the older ones who opened the way,

the conversations that don' t end, and a world that will let Ella Nachimovitz

(born January 2014) bloom to her fullest

CONTENTS

Men Explain Things to Me   1

The Longest War   19

Worlds Collide in a Luxury Suite: Some Thoughts on
the IMF, Global Injustice, and a Stranger on a Train   39

In Praise of the Threat:
What Marriage Equality Really Means   55

Grandmother Spider   63

Woolf's Darkness: Embracing the Inexplicable   79

Cassandra Among the Creeps   103

#YesAllWomen: Feminists Rewrite the Story   121

Pandora's Box and the Volunteer Police Force   139

Image Credits   155

Acknowledgments   157

CHAPTER 1

Men Explain Things to Me

2008

I still don't know why Sallie and I bothered to go to that party in the forest slope above Aspen. The people were all older than us and dull in a distinguished way, old enough that we, at forty-ish, passed as the occasion's young ladies. The house was great—if you like Ralph Lauren–style chalets—a rugged luxury cabin at 9,000 feet complete with elk antlers, lots of kilims, and a wood-burning stove. We were preparing to leave, when our host said, "No, stay a little longer so I can talk to you." He was an imposing man who'd made a lot of money.

He kept us waiting while the other guests drifted out into

the summer night, and then sat us down at his authentically
grainy wood table and said to me, "So? I hear you've written a
couple of books."

I replied, "Several, actually."

He said, in the way you encourage your friend's seven-
year-old to describe flute practice, "And what are they about?"

They were actually about quite a few different things, the six
or seven out by then, but I began to speak only of the most recent
on that summer day in 2003, *River of Shadows: Eadweard Muybridge and
the Technological Wild West*, my book on the annihilation of time and
space and the industrialization of everyday life.

He cut me off soon after I mentioned Muybridge. "And
have you heard about the *very important* Muybridge book that
came out this year?"

So caught up was I in my assigned role as ingénue that I was
perfectly willing to entertain the possibility that another book
on the same subject had come out simultaneously and I'd somehow missed it. He was already telling me about the very important book—with that smug look I know so well in a man holding
forth, eyes fixed on the fuzzy far horizon of his own authority.

Here, let me just say that my life is well sprinkled with
lovely men, with a long succession of editors who have, since I
was young, listened to and encouraged and published me, with
my infinitely generous younger brother, with splendid friends
of whom it could be said—like the Clerk in *The Canterbury Tales* I

still remember from Mr. Pelen's class on Chaucer—"gladly would he learn and gladly teach." Still, there are these other men, too. So, Mr. Very Important was going on smugly about this book I should have known when Sallie interrupted him, to say, "That's her book." Or tried to interrupt him anyway.

But he just continued on his way. She had to say, "That's her book" three or four times before he finally took it in. And then, as if in a nineteenth-century novel, he went ashen. That I was indeed the author of the very important book it turned out he hadn't read, just read about in the *New York Times Book Review* a few months earlier, so confused the neat categories into which his world was sorted that he was stunned speechless—for a moment, before he began holding forth again. Being women, we were politely out of earshot before we started laughing, and we've never really stopped.

I like incidents of that sort, when forces that are usually so sneaky and hard to point out slither out of the grass and are as obvious as, say, an anaconda that's eaten a cow or an elephant turd on the carpet.

THE SLIPPERY SLOPE OF SILENCINGS

Yes, people of both genders pop up at events to hold forth on irrelevant things and conspiracy theories, but the out-and-out confrontational confidence of the totally ignorant is, in my experience, gendered. Men explain things to me, and other women, whether or not they know what they're talking about. Some men.

Every woman knows what I'm talking about. It's the presumption that makes it hard, at times, for any woman in any field; that keeps women from speaking up and from being heard when they dare; that crushes young women into silence by indicating, the way harassment on the street does, that this is not their world. It trains us in self-doubt and self-limitation just as it exercises men's unsupported overconfidence.

I wouldn't be surprised if part of the trajectory of American politics since 2001 was shaped by, say, the inability to hear Coleen Rowley, the FBI woman who issued those early warnings about al-Qaeda, and it was certainly shaped by a Bush administration to which you couldn't tell anything, including that Iraq had no links to al-Qaeda and no WMDs, or that the war was not going to be a "cakewalk." (Even male experts couldn't penetrate the fortress of its smugness.)

Arrogance might have had something to do with the war, but this syndrome is a war that nearly every woman faces every day, a war within herself too, a belief in her superfluity, an invitation to silence, one from which a fairly nice career as a writer (with a lot of research and facts correctly deployed) has not entirely freed me. After all, there was a moment there when

I was willing to let Mr. Important and his overweening confidence bowl over my more shaky certainty.

Don't forget that I've had a lot more confirmation of my right to think and speak than most women, and I've learned that a certain amount of self-doubt is a good tool for correcting, understanding, listening, and progressing—though too much is paralyzing and total self-confidence produces arrogant idiots. There's a happy medium between these poles to which the genders have been pushed, a warm equatorial belt of give and take where we should all meet.

More extreme versions of our situation exist in, for example, those Middle Eastern countries where women's testimony has no legal standing: so that a woman can't testify that she was raped without a male witness to counter the male rapist. Which there rarely is.

Credibility is a basic survival tool. When I was very young and just beginning to get what feminism was about and why it was necessary, I had a boyfriend whose uncle was a nuclear physicist. One Christmas, he was telling—as though it were a light and amusing subject—how a neighbor's wife in his suburban bomb-making community had come running out of her house naked in the middle of the night screaming that her husband was trying to kill her. How, I asked, did you know that he wasn't trying to kill her? He explained, patiently, that they were respectable middle-class people. Therefore, her-husband-try-

ing-to-kill-her was simply not a credible explanation for her
fleeing the house yelling that her husband was trying to kill her.
That she was crazy, on the other hand....

Even getting a restraining order—a fairly new legal tool—
requires acquiring the credibility to convince the courts that
some guy is a menace and then getting the cops to enforce it.
Restraining orders often don't work anyway. Violence is one
way to silence people, to deny their voice and their credibility,
to assert your right to control over their right to exist. About
three women a day are murdered by spouses or ex-spouses in
this country. It's one of the main causes of death for pregnant
women in the United States. At the heart of the struggle of
feminism to give rape, date rape, marital rape, domestic violence, and workplace sexual harassment legal standing as
crimes has been the necessity of making women credible and
audible.

I tend to believe that women acquired the status of human
beings when these kinds of acts started to be taken seriously,
when the big things that stop us and kill us were addressed
legally from the mid-1970s on; well after, that is, my birth.
And for anyone about to argue that workplace sexual intimidation isn't a life-or-death issue, remember that Marine Lance
Corporal Maria Lauterbach, age twenty, was apparently killed
by her higher-ranking colleague one winter's night while she
was waiting to testify that he raped her. The burned remains of

her pregnant body were found in the fire pit in his backyard.

Being told that, categorically, he knows what he's talking about and she doesn't, however minor a part of any given conversation, perpetuates the ugliness of this world and holds back its light. After my book *Wanderlust* came out in 2000, I found myself better able to resist being bullied out of my own perceptions and interpretations. On two occasions around that time, I objected to the behavior of a man, only to be told that the incidents hadn't happened at all as I said, that I was subjective, delusional, overwrought, dishonest—in a nutshell, female.

Most of my life, I would have doubted myself and backed down. Having public standing as a writer of history helped me stand my ground, but few women get that boost, and billions of women must be out there on this seven-billion-person planet being told that they are not reliable witnesses to their own lives, that the truth is not their property, now or ever. This goes way beyond Men Explaining Things, but it's part of the same archipelago of arrogance.

Men explain things to me, still. And no man has ever apologized for explaining, wrongly, things that I know and they don't. Not yet, but according to the actuarial tables, I may have another forty-something years to live, more or less, so it could happen. Though I'm not holding my breath.

WOMEN FIGHTING ON TWO FRONTS

A few years after the idiot in Aspen, I was in Berlin giving a talk when the Marxist writer Tariq Ali invited me out to a dinner that included a male writer and translator and three women a little younger than me who would remain deferential and mostly silent throughout the dinner. Tariq was great. Perhaps the translator was peeved that I insisted on playing a modest role in the conversation, but when I said something about how Women Strike for Peace, the extraordinary, little-known anti-nuclear and antiwar group founded in 1961, helped bring down the communist-hunting House Committee on Un-American Activities, HUAC, Mr. Very Important II sneered at me. HUAC, he insisted, didn't exist by the early 1960s and, anyway, no women's group played such a role in HUAC's downfall. His scorn was so withering, his confidence so aggressive, that arguing with him seemed a scary exercise in futility and an invitation to more insult.

I think I was at nine books at that point, including one that drew from primary documents about and interviews with a key member of Women Strike for Peace. But explaining men still assume I am, in some sort of obscene impregnation metaphor, an empty vessel to be filled with their wisdom and knowledge. A Freudian would claim to know what they have and I lack, but intelligence is not situated in the crotch—even if you can write one of Virginia Woolf's long mellifluous musical sentences about the subtle subjugation of women in the snow with your willie. Back in my hotel room, I searched online a bit and found that Eric Bentley in his definitive history of the House Committee on Un-American Activities credits Women Strike for Peace with "striking the crucial blow in the fall of HUAC's Bastille." In the early 1960s.

So I opened an essay (on Jane Jacobs, Betty Friedan, and Rachel Carson) for the *Nation* with this interchange, in part as a shout-out to one of the more unpleasant men who have explained things to me: Dude, if you're reading this, you're a carbuncle on the face of humanity and an obstacle to civilization. Feel the shame.

The battle with Men Who Explain Things has trampled down many women—of my generation, of the up-and-coming generation we need so badly, here and in Pakistan and Bolivia and Java, not to speak of the countless women who came before me and were not allowed into the laboratory, or the library, or the conversation, or the revolution, or even the category called human.

After all, Women Strike for Peace was founded by women who were tired of making the coffee and doing the typing and not having any voice or decision-making role in the antinuclear movement of the 1950s. Most women fight wars on two fronts, one for whatever the putative topic is and one simply for the right to speak, to have ideas, to be acknowledged to be in possession of facts and truths, to have value, to be a human being. Things have gotten better, but this war won't end in my lifetime. I'm still fighting it, for myself certainly, but also for all those younger women who have something to say, in the hope that they will get to say it.

POSTSCRIPT

One evening over dinner in March 2008, I began to joke, as I often had before, about writing an essay called "Men Explain Things to Me." Every writer has a stable of ideas that never make it to the racetrack, and I'd been trotting this pony out recreationally once in a while. My houseguest, the brilliant theorist and activist Marina Sitrin, insisted that I had to write it down because people like her younger sister Sam needed to read it. Young women, she said, needed to know that being belittled wasn't the result of their own secret failings; it was the boring old gender wars, and it happened to most of us who were female at some point or other.

I wrote it in one sitting early the next morning. When something assembles itself that fast, it's clear it's been composing itself somewhere in the unknowable back of the mind for a long time. It wanted to be written; it was restless for the racetrack; it galloped along once I sat down at the computer. Since Marina slept in later than me in those days, I served it for breakfast and later that day sent it to Tom Engelhardt at TomDispatch, who published it online soon after. It spread quickly, as essays put up at Tom's site do, and has never stopped going around, being reposted and shared and commented upon. It's circulated like nothing else I've done.

It struck a chord. And a nerve.

Some men explained why men explaining things to women wasn't really a gendered phenomenon. Usually, women then pointed out that, in insisting on their right to dismiss the experiences women say they have, men succeeded in explaining in just the way I said they sometimes do. (For the record, I do believe that women have explained things in patronizing ways, to men among others. But that's not indicative of the massive power differential that takes far more sinister forms as well or of the broad pattern of how gender works in our society.)

Other men got it and were cool. This was, after all, written in the era when male feminists had become a more meaningful presence, and feminism was funnier than ever. Not everyone knew they were funny, however. At TomDispatch in 2008, I got an email from an older man in Indianapolis, who wrote in to tell me that he had "never personally or professionally shortchanged a woman" and went on to berate me for not hanging out with "more regular guys or at least do a little homework first." He then gave me some advice about how to run my life and commented on my "feelings of inferiority." He thought that being patronized was an experience a woman chooses to have, or could choose not to have—and so the fault was all mine.

A website named "Academic Men Explain Things to Me" arose, and hundreds of university women shared their stories of being patronized, belittled, talked over, and more. The term "mansplaining" was coined soon after the piece appeared, and I was sometimes credited with it. In fact, I had nothing to do with its actual creation, though my essay, along with all the men who embodied the idea, apparently inspired it. (I have doubts about the word and don't use it myself much; it seems to me to go a little heavy on the idea that men are inherently flawed this way, rather than that some men explain things they shouldn't and don't hear things they should. If it's not clear enough in the piece, I love it when people explain things to me they know and I'm interested in but don't yet know; it's when they explain things to me I know and they don't that the conversation goes wrong.) By 2012, the term "mansplained"—one of the *New York Times*'s words of the year for 2010—was being used in mainstream political journalism.

Alas, this was because it dovetailed pretty well with the times. TomDispatch reposted "Men Explain Things" in August 2012, and fortuitously, more or less simultaneously, Representative Todd Akin (R-Missouri) made his infamous statement that we don't need abortion for women who are raped, because "if it's a legitimate rape, the female body has ways to try to shut the whole thing down." That electoral season was peppered by the crazy pro-rape, anti-fact statements of male conservatives. And salted with feminists pointing out why feminism is necessary and why these guys are scary. It was nice to be one of the voices in that conversation; the piece had a big revival.

Chords, nerves: the thing is still circulating as I write. The point of the essay was never to suggest that I think I am notably oppressed. It was to take these conversations as the narrow end of the wedge that opens up space for men and closes it off for women, space to speak, to be heard, to have rights, to participate, to be respected, to be a full and free human being. This is one way that, in polite discourse, power is expressed—the same power that in impolite discourse and in physical acts of intimidation and violence, and very often in how the world is organized—silences and erases and annihilates women, as equals, as participants, as human beings with rights, and far too often as living beings.

The battle for women to be treated like human beings with rights to life, liberty, and the pursuit of involvement in cultural and political arenas continues, and it is sometimes a pretty grim battle. I surprised myself when I wrote the essay, which began with an amusing incident and ended with rape and murder. That made clear to me the continuum that stretches from minor social misery to violent silencing and violent death (and I think we would understand misogyny and violence against women even better if we looked at the abuse of power as a whole rather than treating domestic violence separately from rape and murder and harrassment and intimidation, online and at home and in the workplace and in the streets; seen together, the pattern is clear).

Having the right to show up and speak are basic to survival, to dignity, and to liberty. I'm grateful that, after an early life of being silenced, sometimes violently, I grew up to have a voice, circumstances that will always bind me to the rights of the voiceless.

CHAPTER 2

The Longest War

2013

Here in the United States, where there is a reported rape every 6.2 minutes, and one in five women will be raped in her lifetime, the rape and gruesome murder of a young woman on a bus in New Delhi on December 16, 2012, was treated as an exceptional incident. The story of the sexual assault of an unconscious teenager by members of the Steubenville High School football team in Ohio was still unfolding, and gang rapes aren't that unusual here either. Take your pick: some of the twenty men who gang-raped an eleven-year-old in Cleveland, Texas, were sentenced shortly beforehand, while the instigator of the gang rape of a sixteen-year-old in Richmond, California, was sentenced in that fall of 2012 too, and four men who gang-raped a fifteen-year-old near New Orleans were sentenced that April, though the six men who gang-raped a fourteen-year-old in Chicago that year were still at large. Not that I went out looking for incidents: they're everywhere in the news, though no one adds them up and indicates that there might actually be a pattern.

There is, however, a pattern of violence against women that's broad and deep and horrific and incessantly overlooked. Occasionally, a case involving a celebrity or lurid details in a particular case get a lot of attention in the media, but such cases are treated as anomalies, while the abundance of incidental news items about violence against women in this country, in other countries, on every continent including Antarctica, constitute a kind of background wallpaper for the news.

If you'd rather talk about bus rapes than gang rapes, there was the rape of a developmentally disabled woman on a Los Angeles bus that November and the kidnapping of an autistic sixteen-year-old on the regional transit train system in Oakland, California—she was raped repeatedly by her abductor over two days this winter—and a gang rape of multiple women on a bus in Mexico City recently, too. While I was writing this, I read that another female bus rider was kidnapped in India and gang-raped all night by the bus driver and five of his friends who must have thought what happened in New Delhi was awesome.

We have an abundance of rape and violence against women in this country and on this Earth, though it's almost never treated as a civil rights or human rights issue, or a crisis, or even a pattern. Violence doesn't have a race, a class, a religion, or a nationality, but it does have a gender.

Here I want to say one thing: though virtually all the perpetrators of such crimes are men, that doesn't mean all men are violent. Most are not. In addition, men obviously also suffer violence, largely at the hands of other men, and every violent death, every assault is terrible. Women can and do engage in intimate partner violence, but recent studies state that these acts don't often result in significant injury, let alone death; on the other hand, men murdered by their partners are often killed in self-defense, and intimate violence sends a lot of women to the hospital and the grave. But the subject here is the pandemic of violence by men against women, both intimate violence and stranger violence.

WHAT WE DON'T TALK ABOUT WHEN WE DON'T TALK ABOUT GENDER

There's so much of it. We could talk about the assault and rape of a seventy-three-year-old in Manhattan's Central Park in

September 2012, or the recent rape of a four-year-old and an eighty-three-year-old in Louisiana, or the New York City policeman who was arrested in October of 2012 for what appeared to be serious plans to kidnap, rape, cook, and eat a woman, any woman, because the hate wasn't personal (although maybe it was for the San Diego man who actually killed and cooked his wife in November and the man from New Orleans who killed, dismembered, and cooked his girlfriend in 2005).

Those are all exceptional crimes, but we could also talk about quotidian assaults, because though a rape is reported only every 6.2 minutes in this country, the estimated total is perhaps five times as high. Which means that there may be very nearly a rape a minute in the United States. It all adds up to tens of millions of rape victims. A significant portion of the women you know are survivors.

We could talk about high-school and college-athlete rapes, or campus rapes, to which university authorities have been appallingly uninterested in responding in many cases, including that high school in Steubenville, Notre Dame University, Amherst College, and many others. We could talk about the escalating pandemic of rape, sexual assault, and sexual harassment in the US military, where Secretary of Defense Leon Panetta estimated that there were nineteen thousand sexual assaults on fellow soldiers in 2010 alone and that the great majority of assailants got away with it, though four-star general

Jeffrey Sinclair was indicted in September for "a slew of sex crimes against women."

Never mind workplace violence, let's go home. So many men murder their partners and former partners that we have well over a thousand homicides of that kind a year—meaning that every three years the death toll tops 9/11's casualties, though no one declares a war on this particular kind of terror. (Another way to put it: the more than 11,766 corpses from domestic-violence homicides between 9/11 and 2012 exceed the number of deaths of victims on that day *and* all American soldiers killed in the "war on terror.") If we talked about crimes like these and why they are so common, we'd have to talk about what kinds of profound change this society, or this nation, or nearly every nation needs. If we talked about it, we'd be talking about masculinity, or male roles, or maybe patriarchy, and we don't talk much about that.

Instead, we hear that American men commit murder-suicides—at the rate of about twelve a week—because the economy is bad, though they also do it when the economy is good; or that those men in India murdered the bus rider because the poor resent the rich, while other rapes in India are explained by how the rich exploit the poor; and then there are those ever-popular explanations: mental problems and intoxicants—and for jocks, head injuries. The latest spin is that lead exposure was responsible for a lot of our violence, except that both genders are exposed and one commits most of the violence. The pandemic of violence always gets explained as anything but gender, anything but what would seem to be the broadest explanatory pattern of all.

Someone wrote a piece about how white men seem to be the ones who commit mass murders in the United States and the (mostly hostile) commenters only seemed to notice the white part. It's rare that anyone says what this medical study does, even if in the driest way possible: "Being male has been identified as a risk factor for violent criminal behavior in several studies, as have exposure to tobacco smoke before birth, having antisocial parents, and belonging to a poor family."

It's not that I want to pick on men. I just think that if we noticed that women are, on the whole, radically less violent, we might be able to theorize where violence comes from and what we can do about it a lot more productively. Clearly the ready availability of guns is a huge problem for the United States, but despite this availability to everyone, murder is still a crime committed by men 90 percent of the time.

The pattern is plain as day. We could talk about this as a global problem, looking at the epidemic of assault, harassment, and rape of women in Cairo's Tahrir Square that has taken away the freedom they celebrated during the Arab Spring—and led some men there to form defense teams to help counter it—or the persecution of women in public and private in India from "Eve-teasing" to bride-burning, or "honor killings" in South Asia and the Middle East, or the way that South Africa has become a global rape capital, with an estimated six hundred thousand rapes last year, or how rape has been used as a tactic and "weapon" of war in Mali, Sudan, and the Congo, as it was in the former Yugoslavia, or the pervasiveness of rape and harassment in Mexico and the femicide in Juarez, or the denial of basic rights for women in Saudi Arabia and the myriad sexual assaults on immigrant domestic workers there, or the way that the Dominique Strauss-Kahn case in the United States revealed what impunity he and others had in France, and it's only for lack of space I'm leaving out Britain and Canada and Italy (with its ex-prime minister known for his orgies with the underaged), Argentina and Australia and so many other countries.

WHO HAS THE RIGHT TO KILL YOU?

But maybe you're tired of statistics, so let's just talk about a single incident that happened in my city while I was researching this essay in January 2013, one of many local incidents that made the local papers that month in which men assaulted women:

> A woman was stabbed after she rebuffed a man's sexual advances while she walked in San Francisco's Tenderloin neighborhood late Monday night, a police spokesman said today. The 33-year-old victim was walking down the street when a stranger approached her and propositioned her, po-

lice spokesman Officer Albie Esparza said. When she rejected him, the man became very upset and slashed the victim in the face and stabbed her in the arm, Esparza said.

The man, in other words, framed the situation as one in which his chosen victim had no rights and liberties, while he had the right to control and punish her. This should remind us that violence is first of all authoritarian. It begins with this premise: I have the right to control you.

Murder is the extreme version of that authoritarianism, where the murderer asserts he has the right to decide whether you live or die, the ultimate means of controlling someone. This may be true even if you are obedient, because the desire to control comes out of a rage that obedience can't assuage. Whatever fears, whatever sense of vulnerability may underlie such behavior, it also comes out of entitlement, the entitlement to inflict suffering and even death on other people. It breeds misery in the perpetrator and the victims.

As for that incident in my city, similar things happen all the time. Many versions of it happened to me when I was younger, sometimes involving death threats and often involving torrents of obscenities: a man approaches a woman with both desire and the furious expectation that the desire will likely be rebuffed. The fury and desire come in a package, all twisted together into something that always threatens to turn *eros* into *thanatos*, love into death, sometimes literally.

It's a system of control. It's why so many intimate-partner murders are of women who dared to break up with those partners. As a result, it imprisons a lot of women, and though you could say that the Tenderloin attacker on January 7, or a brutal would-be-rapist near my own neighborhood on January 5, or another rapist here on January 12, or the San Franciscan who on January 6 set his girlfriend on fire for refusing to do his laundry, or the guy who was just sentenced to 370 years for some particularly violent rapes in San Francisco in late 2011, were marginal characters, rich, famous, and privileged guys do it, too.

The Japanese vice-consul in San Francisco was charged with twelve felony counts of spousal abuse and assault with a deadly weapon in September 2012, the same month that, in the same town, the ex-girlfriend of Mason Mayer (brother of Yahoo CEO Marissa Mayer) testified in court: "He ripped out my earrings, tore my eyelashes off, while spitting in my face and telling me how unlovable I am . . . I was on the ground in the fetal position, and when I tried to move, he squeezed both knees tighter into my sides to restrain me and slapped me." According to *San Francisco Chronicle* reporter Vivian Ho, she also testified that "Mayer slammed her head onto the floor repeatedly and pulled out clumps of her hair, telling her that the only way she was leaving the apartment alive was if he drove her to the Golden Gate Bridge 'where you can jump off or I will push you off.'" Mason Mayer got probation.

The summer before, an estranged husband violated his wife's restraining order against him, shooting her—and killing or wounding six other women—at her workplace in suburban Milwaukee, but since there were only four corpses the crime was largely overlooked in the media in a year with so many more spectacular mass murders in this country (and we still haven't really talked about the fact that, of sixty-two mass shootings in the United States in three decades, only one was by a woman, because when you say *lone gunman*, everyone talks about loners and guns but not about men—and by the way, nearly two-thirds of all women killed by guns are killed by their partner or ex-partner).

What's love got to do with it, asked Tina Turner, whose ex-husband Ike once said, "Yeah I hit her, but I didn't hit her more than the average guy beats his wife." A woman is beaten every nine seconds in this country. Just to be clear: not nine minutes, but nine seconds. It's the number-one cause of injury to American women; of the two million injured annually, more than half a million of those injuries require medical attention while about 145,000 require overnight hospitalizations, according to the Center for Disease Control, and you don't want to know about the dentistry needed afterwards. Spouses are also the leading cause of death for pregnant women in the United States.

THE CHASM BETWEEN OUR WORLDS

Rape and other acts of violence, up to and including murder, as well as threats of violence, constitute the barrage some men lay down as they attempt to control some women, and fear of that violence limits most women in ways they've gotten so used to they hardly notice—and we hardly address. There are exceptions: last summer someone wrote to me to describe a college class in which the students were asked what they do to stay safe from rape. The young women described the intricate ways they stayed alert, limited their access to the world, took precautions, and essentially thought about rape all the time (while the young men in the class, he added, gaped in astonishment). The chasm between their worlds had briefly and suddenly become visible.

Mostly, however, we don't talk about it—though a graphic has been circulating on the Internet called "Ten Top Tips to End Rape," the kind of thing young women get often enough, but this one had a subversive twist. It offered advice like this: "Carry a whistle! If you are worried you might assault someone 'by accident' you can hand it to the person you are with, so they can call for help." While funny, the piece points out something terrible: the usual guidelines in such situations put the full burden of prevention on potential victims, treating the violence as a given. There's no good reason (and many bad reasons) colleges spend more time telling women how to survive predators than telling the other half of their students not to be predators.

Threats of sexual assault now seem to take place online regularly. In late 2011, British columnist Laurie Penny wrote,

> An opinion, it seems, is the short skirt of the Internet. Having one and flaunting it is somehow asking an amorphous mass of almost-entirely male keyboard-bashers to tell you how they'd like to rape, kill, and urinate on you. This week, after a particularly ugly slew of threats, I decided to make just a few of those messages public on Twitter, and the response I received was overwhelming. Many could not believe the hate I received, and many more began to share their own stories of harassment, intimidation, and abuse.

Women in the online gaming community have been harassed, threatened, and driven out. Anita Sarkeesian, a feminist media critic who documented such incidents, received support for her work, but also, in the words of a journalist, "another wave of really aggressive, you know, violent personal threats, her accounts attempted to be hacked. And one man in Ontario took the step of making an online video game where you could punch Anita's image on the screen. And if you punched it multiple times, bruises and cuts would appear on her image." The difference between these online gamers and the Taliban men who, last October, tried to murder fourteen-year-old Malala Yousafzai for speaking out about the right of Pakistani women to education is one of degree. Both are trying to silence and punish women for claiming voice, power, and the right to participate. Welcome to Manistan.

THE PARTY FOR THE PROTECTION OF THE RIGHTS OF RAPISTS

It's not just public, or private, or online either. It's also embedded in our political system, and our legal system, which before feminists fought for us didn't recognize most domestic violence, or sexual harassment and stalking, or date rape, or acquaintance rape, or marital rape, and in cases of rape still often tries the victim rather than the rapist, as though only perfect maidens could be assaulted—or believed.

As we learned in the 2012 election campaign, it's also embedded in the minds and mouths of our politicians. Remember that spate of crazy pro-rape things Republican men said last summer and fall, starting with Todd Akin's notorious claim that a woman has ways of preventing pregnancy in cases of rape, a statement he made in order to deny women control over their own bodies (in the form of access to abortion after rape). After that, of course, Senate candidate Richard Mourdock claimed that rape pregnancies were "a gift from God," and soon after another Republican politician piped up to defend Akin's comment.

Happily the five publicly pro-rape Republicans in the 2012

campaign all lost their election bids. (Stephen Colbert tried to warn them that women had gotten the vote in 1920.) But it's not just a matter of the garbage they say (and the price they now pay). Congressional Republicans refused to reauthorize the Violence Against Women Act because they objected to the protection it gave immigrants, transgender women, and Native American women. (Speaking of epidemics, one of three Native American women will be raped, and on the reservations 88 percent of those rapes are by non-Native men who know tribal governments can't prosecute them. So much for rape as a crime of passion—these are crimes of calculation and opportunism.)

And they're out to gut reproductive rights—birth control as well as abortion, as they've pretty effectively done in many states over the last dozen years. What's meant by "reproductive rights," of course, is the right of women to control their own bodies. Didn't I mention earlier that violence against women is a control issue?

And though rapes are often investigated lackadaisically—there is a backlog of about four hundred thousand untested rape kits in this country—rapists who impregnate their victims have parental rights in thirty-one states. Oh, and former vice-presidential candidate and current congressman Paul Ryan (R-Manistan) is reintroducing a bill that would give states the right to ban abortions and might even conceivably allow a rapist to sue his victim for having one.

ALL THE THINGS THAT AREN'T TO BLAME

Of course, women are capable of all sorts of major unpleasant-
ness, and there are violent crimes by women, but the so-called
war of the sexes is extraordinarily lopsided when it comes to actual violence. Unlike the last (male) head of the International
Monetary Fund, the current (female) head is not going to assault an employee at a luxury hotel; top-ranking female officers
in the US military, unlike their male counterparts, are not accused of any sexual assaults; and young female athletes, unlike
those male football players in Steubenville, aren't likely to uri-
nate on unconscious boys, let alone violate them and boast
about it in YouTube videos and Twitter feeds.

No female bus riders in India have ganged up to sexually
assault a man so badly he dies of his injuries, nor are maraud-
ing packs of women terrorizing men in Cairo's Tahrir Square,
and there's just no maternal equivalent to the 11 percent of
rapes that are by fathers or stepfathers. Of the people in
prison in the United States, 93.5 percent are not women, and
though quite a lot of the prisoners should not be there in the
first place, maybe some of them should because of violence,
until we think of a better way to deal with it, and them.

No major female pop star has blown the head off a young
man she took home with her, as did Phil Spector. (He is now part
of that 93.5 percent for the shotgun slaying of Lana Clarkson,

apparently for refusing his advances.) No female action-movie star has been charged with domestic violence, because Angelina Jolie just isn't doing what Mel Gibson and Steve McQueen did, and there aren't any celebrated female movie directors who gave a thriteen-year-old drugs before sexually assaulting that child, while she kept saying "no," as did Roman Polanski.

IN MEMORY OF JYOTI SINGH

What's the matter with manhood? There's something about how masculinity is imagined, about what's praised and encouraged, about the way violence is passed on to boys that needs to be addressed. There are lovely and wonderful men out there, and one of the things that's encouraging in this round of the war against women is how many men I've seen who get it, who think it's their issue too, who stand up for us and with us in everyday life, online and in the marches from New Delhi to San Francisco this winter.

Increasingly men are becoming good allies—and there always have been some. Kindness and gentleness never had a gender, and neither did empathy. Domestic violence statistics are down significantly from earlier decades (even though they're still shockingly high), and a lot of men are at work crafting new ideas and ideals about masculinity and power.

Gay men have redefined and occasionally undermined conventional masculinity—publicly, for many decades—and often been great allies for women. Women's liberation has often been portrayed as a movement intent on encroaching upon or taking power and privilege away from men, as though in some dismal zero-sum game, only one gender at a time could be free and powerful. But we are free together or slaves together. Surely the mindset of those who think they need to win, to dominate, to punish, to reign supreme must be terrible and far from free, and giving up this unachievable pursuit would be liberatory.

There are other things I'd rather write about, but this affects everything else. The lives of half of humanity are still dogged by, drained by, and sometimes ended by this pervasive variety of violence. Think of how much more time and energy we would have to focus on other things that matter if we weren't so busy surviving. Look at it this way: one of the best journalists I know is afraid to walk home at night in our neighborhood. Should she stop working late? How many women have had to stop doing their work, or been stopped from doing it, for similar reasons? It's clear now that monumental harrassment online keeps many women from speaking up and writing altogether.

One of the most exciting new political movements on Earth is the Native Canadian indigenous rights movement, with feminist and environmental overtones, called Idle No More. On December 27, shortly after the movement took off, a Native woman was kidnapped, raped, beaten, and left for dead in Thunder Bay, Ontario, by men whose remarks framed the crime as retaliation against Idle No More. Afterward, she walked four hours through the bitter cold and survived to tell her tale. Her assailants, who have threatened to do it again, are still at large.

The New Delhi rape and murder of Jyoti Singh, the twenty-three-year-old who was studying physiotherapy so that she could better herself while helping others, and the assault on her male companion (who survived) seem to have triggered the reaction that we have needed for one hundred, or one thousand, or five thousand years. May she be to women—and men—worldwide what Emmett Till, murdered by white supremacists in 1955, was to African Americans and the then-nascent US civil rights movement.

We have far more than eighty-seven thousand rapes in this country every year, but each of them is invariably portrayed as an isolated incident. We have dots so close they're splatters melting into a stain, but hardly anyone connects them, or names that stain. In India they did. They said that this is a civil rights issue, it's a human rights issue, it's everyone's problem, it's not isolated, and it's never going to be acceptable again. It has to change. It's your job to change it, and mine, and ours.

CHAPTER 3

Worlds Collide
in a Luxury Suite

SOME THOUGHTS ON THE IMF, GLOBAL INJUSTICE,

AND A STRANGER ON A TRAIN

2011

How can I tell a story we already know too well? Her name was Africa. His was France. He colonized her, exploited her, silenced her, and even decades after it was supposed to have ended, still acted with a high hand in resolving her affairs in places like Côte d'Ivoire, a name she had been given because of her export products, not her own identity.

Her name was Asia. His was Europe. Her name was silence. His was power. Her name was poverty. His was wealth. Her name was Her, but what was hers? His name was His, and he presumed everything was his, including her, and he thought he could take her without asking and without consequences. It was a very old story, though its outcome had been changing a little in recent decades. And this time around the consequences are shaking a lot of foundations, all of which clearly needed shaking.

Who would ever write a fable as obvious, as heavy-handed as the story we've just been given? The extraordinarily powerful head of the International Monetary Fund (IMF), a global organization that has created mass poverty and economic injustice, allegedly assaulted a hotel maid, an immigrant from Africa, in a hotel's luxury suite in New York City.

Worlds have collided. In an earlier era, her word would have been worthless against his and she might not have filed charges, or the police might not have followed through and yanked Dominique Strauss-Kahn off a plane to Paris at the last moment. But she did, and they did, and now he's in custody, and the economy of Europe has been dealt a blow, and French politics have been upended, and that nation is reeling and soul-searching.

What were they thinking, these men who decided to give him this singular position of power, despite all the stories and evidence of such viciousness? What was he thinking when he decided he could get away with it? Did he think he was in France, where apparently he did get away with it? Only now is a young woman who says he assaulted her in 2002 pressing charges—her own politician mother talked her out of it, and she worried about the impact it could have on her journalistic career (while her mother was apparently worrying more about *his* career).

And the *Guardian* reports that these stories "have added weight to claims by Piroska Nagy, a Hungarian-born economist, that the fund's director engaged in sustained harassment when she was working at the IMF that left her feeling she had little choice but to agree to sleep with him at the World Economic Forum in Davos in January 2008. She alleged he persistently called and emailed on the pretext of asking questions about [her expertise,] Ghana's economy, but then used sexual language and asked her out."

In some accounts, the woman Strauss-Kahn is charged with assaulting in New York is from Ghana, in others a Muslim from nearby Guinea. "Ghana—Prisoner of the IMF" ran a headline in 2001 by the usually mild-mannered BBC. Its report documented the way the IMF's policies had destroyed that rice-growing nation's food security, opening it up to cheap imported US rice, and plunging the country's majority into dire poverty. Everything became a commodity for which you had to pay, from using a toilet to getting a bucket of water, and many could not pay. Perhaps it would be too perfect if she was a refugee from the IMF's policies in Ghana. Guinea, on the other hand, liberated itself from the IMF management thanks to the discovery of major oil reserves, but remains a country of severe corruption and economic disparity.

PIMPING FOR THE GLOBAL NORTH

There's an axiom evolutionary biologists used to like: "ontogeny recapitulates phylogeny," or the development of the embryonic individual repeats that of its species' evolution. Does the ontogeny of this alleged assault echo the phylogeny of the International Monetary Fund? After all, the organization was founded late in World War II as part of the notorious Bretton Woods conference that would impose American economic visions on the rest of the world.

The IMF was meant to be a lending institution to help countries develop, but by the 1980s it had become an organization with an ideology—free trade and free-market fundamentalism. It used its loans to gain enormous power over the economies and policies of nations throughout the global South.

However, if the IMF gained power throughout the 1990s, it began losing that power in the twenty-first century, thanks to effective popular resistance to the economic policies it embodied and the economic collapse such policies produced. Strauss-Kahn was brought in to salvage the wreckage of an organization that, in 2008, had to sell off its gold reserves and reinvent its mission.

Her name was Africa. His name was IMF. He set her up to be pillaged, to go without health care, to starve. He laid waste to her to enrich his friends. Her name was Global South. His name was Washington Consensus. But his winning streak was running out and her star was rising.

It was the IMF that created the economic conditions that destroyed the Argentinian economy by 2001, and it was the revolt against the IMF (among other neoliberal forces) that prompted Latin America's rebirth over the past decade. Whatever you think of Hugo Chávez, it was loans from oil-rich Venezuela that allowed Argentina to pay off its IMF loans early so that it could set its own saner economic policies.

The IMF was a predatory force, opening developing countries up to economic assaults from the wealthy North and powerful transnational corporations. It was a pimp. Maybe it still is. But since the Seattle anticorporate demonstrations of 1999 set a global movement alight, there has been a revolt against it, and those forces have won in Latin America, changing the framework of all economic debates to come and enriching our imaginations when it comes to economies and possibilities.

Today, the IMF is a mess, the World Trade Organization largely sidelined, NAFTA almost universally reviled, the Free Trade Area of the Americas canceled (though bilateral free-trade agreements continue), and much of the world has learned a great deal from the decade's crash course in economic policy.

STRANGERS ON A TRAIN

The *New York Times* reported it this way: "As the impact of Mr. Strauss-Kahn's predicament hit home, others, including some in the news media, began to reveal accounts, long suppressed or anonymous, of what they called Mr. Strauss-Kahn's previously predatory behavior toward women and his aggressive sexual pursuit of them, from students and journalists to subordinates."

In other words, he created an atmosphere that was uncomfortable or dangerous for women, which would be one thing if he were working in, say, a small office. But that a man who controls some part of the fate of the world apparently devoted his energies to generating fear, misery, and injustice around him says something about the shape of our world and the values of the nations and institutions that tolerated his behavior and that of men like him.

The United States has not been short on sex scandals of late, and they reek of the same arrogance, but they were at least consensual (as far as we know). The head of the IMF is charged with sexual assault. If that term confuses you take out the word "sexual" and just focus on "assault," on violence, on the refusal to treat someone as a human being, on the denial of the most basic of human rights, the right to bodily integrity and self-determination. "The rights of man" was one of the great phrases of the French Revolution, but it's always been questionable whether it included the rights of women.

The United States has a hundred million flaws, but I am proud that the police believed this woman and that she will have her day in court. I am gratified this time not to be in a country that has decided that the career of a powerful man or the fate of an international institution matters more than this woman and her rights and well-being. This is what we mean by democracy: that everyone has a voice, that no one gets away with things just because of their wealth, power, race, or gender.

Two days before Strauss-Kahn allegedly emerged from that hotel bathroom naked, there was a big demonstration in New York City. "Make Wall Street Pay" was the theme and union workers, radicals, the unemployed, and more—twenty thousand people—gathered to protest the economic assault in this country that is creating such suffering and deprivation for the many—and obscene wealth for the few. (It was the last big New York City economic-justice protest preceding the birth of Occupy Wall Street on September 17, 2011, which had, to say the least, more impact.)

I attended. On the crowded subway car back to Brooklyn afterward, the youngest of my three female companions had her bottom groped by a man about Strauss-Kahn's age. At first, she thought he had simply bumped into her. That was before she felt her buttock being cupped and said something to me, as young women often do, tentatively, quietly, as though it were perhaps not happening or perhaps not quite a problem.

Finally, she glared at him and told him to stop. I was reminded of a moment when I was an impoverished seventeen-year-old living in Paris and some geezer grabbed my ass. It was perhaps my most American moment in France, then the land of a thousand disdainful gropers; American because I was carrying three grapefruits, a precious purchase in my impoverished era, and I threw those grapefruits, one after another, like baseballs at the creep and had the satisfaction of watching him scuttle into the night.

His action, like so much sexual violence against women, was undoubtedly meant to be a reminder that this world was not mine, that my rights—my *liberté*, *egalité*, *sororité*, if you will—didn't matter. Except that I had sent him running in a barrage of fruit. And Dominique Strauss-Kahn got pulled off a plane to answer to justice. Still, that a friend of mine got groped on her way back from a march about justice makes it clear how much there still is to be done.

THE POOR STARVE,
WHILE THE RICH EAT THEIR WORDS

What makes the sex scandal that broke open last week so resonant is the way the alleged assailant and victim model larger relationships around the world, starting with the IMF's assault on
the poor. That assault is part of the great class war of our era,
in which the rich and their proxies in government have endeav-
ored to aggrandize their holdings at the expense of the rest of
us. Poor countries in the developing world paid first, but the
rest of us are paying now, as those policies and the suffering
they impose come home to roost via right-wing economics that
savages unions, education systems, the environment, and pro-
grams for the poor, disabled, and elderly in the name of priva-
tization, free markets, and tax cuts.

In one of the more remarkable apologies of our era, Bill
Clinton—who had his own sex scandal once upon a time—told
the United Nations on World Food Day in October 2008, as
the global economy was melting down:

> We need the World Bank, the IMF, all the big foundations,
> and all the governments to admit that, for 30 years, we all
> blew it, including me when I was President. We were wrong to
> believe that food was like some other product in interna-
> tional trade, and we all have to go back to a more responsible
> and sustainable form of agriculture.

He said it even more bluntly last year:

Since 1981, the United States has followed a policy, until
the last year or so when we started rethinking it, that we rich
countries that produce a lot of food should sell it to poor
countries and relieve them of the burden of producing
their own food, so, thank goodness, they can leap directly
into the industrial era. It has not worked. It may have been
good for some of my farmers in Arkansas, but it has not
worked. It was a mistake. It was a mistake that I was a party
to. I am not pointing the finger at anybody. I did that. I
have to live every day with the consequences of the lost capacity to produce a rice crop in Haiti to feed those people,
because of what I did.

Clinton's admissions were on a level with former Federal
Reserve chairman Alan Greenspan's 2008 admission that the
premise of his economic politics was wrong. The former policies and those of the IMF, World Bank, and free-trade funda-
mentalists had created poverty, suffering, hunger, and death.
We have learned, most of us, and the world *has* changed re-
markably since the day when those who opposed free-market
fundamentalism were labeled "flat-earth advocates, protec-
tionist trade unions, and yuppies looking for their 1960's fix,"
in the mortal words of Thomas Friedman, later eaten.

A remarkable thing happened after the devastating Haitian
earthquake last year: the IMF under Strauss-Kahn planned to

use the vulnerability of that country to force new loans on it with the usual terms. Activists reacted to a plan guaranteed to increase the indebtedness of a nation already crippled by the kind of neoliberal policies for which Clinton belatedly apologized. The IMF blinked, stepped back, and agreed to cancel Haiti's existing debt to the organization. It was a remarkable victory for informed activism.

POWERS OF THE POWERLESS

It looks as though a hotel maid may end the career of one of the most powerful men in the world, or rather that he will have ended it himself by discounting the rights and humanity of that worker. Pretty much the same thing happened to Meg Whitman, the former eBay billionaire who ran for governor of California last year. She leapt on the conservative bandwagon by attacking undocumented immigrants—until it turned out that she had herself long employed one, Nicky Diaz, as a housekeeper.

When, after nine years, it had become politically inconvenient to keep Diaz around, she fired the woman abruptly, claimed she'd never known her employee was undocumented, and refused to pay her final wages. In other words, Whitman was willing to spend $178 million on her campaign, but may have brought herself down thanks, in part, to $6,210 in unpaid wages.

Diaz said, "I felt like she was throwing me away like a piece of garbage." The garbage had a voice, the California Nurses Union amplified it, and California was spared domination by a billionaire whose policies would have further brutalized the poor and impoverished the middle class.

The struggles for justice of an undocumented housekeeper and an immigrant hotel maid are microcosms of the great world war of our time. If Nicky Diaz and the battle over last year's IMF loans to Haiti demonstrate anything, it's that the outcome is uncertain. Sometimes we win the skirmishes, but the war continues. So much remains to be known about what happened in that expensive hotel suite in Manhattan last week, but what we do know is this: a genuine class war is being fought openly in our time, and last week, a so-called socialist put himself on the wrong side of it.

His name was privilege, but hers was possibility. His was the same old story, but hers was a new one about the possibility of changing a story that remains unfinished, that includes all of us, that matters so much, that we will watch but also make and tell in the weeks, months, years, decades to come.

POSTSCRIPT

This essay was written in response to the initial reports of what happened in Dominique Strauss-Kahn's Manhattan hotel room. Afterward, through the massive application of money to powerful teams of lawyers, he was able to get the New York prosecutors to drop the criminal case—and malign his victim's reputation with information his lawyers provided. Like many very poor people and people from countries in turmoil, Nafissatou Diallo had lived in the margins, where telling the truth to authorities is not always a wise or safe thing to do, so she was portrayed as a liar. In a *Newsweek* interview, she said that she had been hesitant to come forward with her rape charges and fearful of the consequences. She had come out of silence and shadows.

Like other women and girls who've been raped, particularly those whose stories threaten the status quo, her character was put on trial. Front-page headlines in the *New York Post*, the local Rupert Murdoch–owned tabloid, claimed that she was a prostitute, though why a prostitute worked full-time as a union hotel maid for $25 an hour was hard to explain, so no one bothered. (The *Post* was obliged to settle after she brought a libel lawsuit.)

People—notably Edward Jay Epstein in the *New York Review of Books*—formulated elaborate stories to explain away what happened. Why had a woman who witnesses said was very upset told a story of being sexually assaulted, why had the alleged assailant attempted to flee the country in an apparent panic, and why was his semen found on her clothing and elsewhere, confirming that a sexual encounter had taken place? There was either a consensual or a nonconsensual sexual encounter. The simplest and most coherent explanation was Diallo's. As Christopher Dickey wrote in the *Daily Beast*, Strauss-Kahn "claims that his less-than-seven-minute sexual encounter with this woman he'd never met before was consensual. To believe him, you'd have to buy the line that Diallo took one look at his potbellied, 60-something naked body fresh out of the shower and just volunteered to go down on her knees."

Afterward, other women came forward to testify about being assaulted by Strauss-Kahn, including a young French journalist who said he tried to rape her. He was implicated in a sex-party ring whose interactions with prostitutes violated French law: as I write he's facing charges for "aggravated pimping," though rape charges brought by a sex worker were dropped.

What matters, in the end, is that a poor immigrant woman upended the career of one of the most powerful men in the world, or rather exposed behavior that should have ended it far earlier. As a result, French women reassessed the misogyny of their society. And Ms. Diallo won her case in civil court against the former head of the IMF, though one part of the terms involving what may have been a substantial financial settlement was silence. Which brings us back to where we began.

CHAPTER 4

In Praise
of the Threat

WHAT MARRIAGE EQUALITY REALLY MEANS

2013

For a long time, the advocates of same-sex marriage have been saying that such unions pose no threat, contradicting the conservatives who say such unions are a threat to traditional marriage. Maybe the conservatives are right, and maybe we should celebrate that threat rather than denying it. The marriage of two men or two women doesn't impact any man-and-woman marriage directly. But metaphysically it could.

To understand how, you need to look at what traditional marriage is. And at the ways in which both sides are dissembling:

the advocates by denying, or more likely overlooking the threat, and the conservatives by being coy about what it's a threat to.

Recently, a lot of Americans have swapped the awkward phrase "same-sex marriage" for the term "marriage equality." The phrase is ordinarily employed to mean that same-sex couples will have the rights different-sexed couples do. But it could also mean that marriage is between equals. That's not what traditional marriage was. Throughout much of its history in the West, the laws defining marriage made the husband essentially an owner and the wife a possession. Or the man a boss and the woman a servant or slave.

The British judge William Blackstone wrote in 1765, in his influential commentary on English common law and, later, American law, "By marriage, the husband and wife are one person in law: that is, the very being or legal existence of the woman is suspended during the marriage, or at least is incorporated and consolidated into that of the husband." Under such rules, a woman's life was dependent on the disposition of her husband, and though there were kind as well as unkind husbands then, rights are more reliable than the kindness of someone who holds absolute power over you. And rights were a long way off.

Until Britain's Married Women's Property Acts of 1870 and 1882, everything belonged to the husband; the wife was penniless on her own account, no matter her inheritance or her earnings. Laws against wife beating were passed around that time in both England and the United States but rarely enforced until the 1970s. That domestic violence is now (sometimes) prosecuted hasn't cured the epidemic of such violence in either country.

The novelist Edna O'Brien's recent memoir has some blood-curdling passages about her own journey through what appears to have been a very traditional marriage. Her first husband was withering about her literary success and obliged her to sign over her checks to him. When she refused to sign over a large film-rights check, he throttled her, but when she went to the police they were not much interested. The violence horrifies me, but so does the underlying assumption that the abuser has the right to control and punish his victim and the way such violence is used to that end.

The Cleveland, Ohio, case of Ariel Castro, accused in 2013 of imprisoning, torturing, and sexually abusing three young women for a decade, is extreme, but it may not be quite the anomaly it is portrayed as. For one thing, Castro, it is claimed, was spectacularly and openly violent to his now-deceased common-law wife. And what lay behind Castro's alleged actions must have been a desire for a situation in which he held absolute power and the women were absolutely powerless, a vicious version of the traditional arrangement.

This is the tradition feminism protested and protests against—not only the extremes but the quotidian situation. Feminists in the nineteenth century made some inroads, those of the 1970s and 1980s made a great many more, which every woman in the United States and UK has benefited from. And feminism made same-sex marriage possible by doing so much to transform a hierarchical relationship into an egalitarian one. Because a marriage between two people of the same gender is inherently egalitarian—one partner may happen to have more power in any number of ways, but for the most part it's a relationship between people who have equal standing and so are free to define their roles themselves.

Gay men and lesbians have already opened up the question of what qualities and roles are male and female in ways that can be liberating for straight people. When they marry, the meaning of marriage is likewise opened up. No hierarchical tradition underlies their union. Some people have greeted this with joy. A Presbyterian pastor who had performed a number of such marriages told me, "I remember coming to this realization when I was meeting with same-sex couples before performing their ceremonies when it was legal in California. The old patriarchal default settings did not apply in their relationships, and it was a glorious thing to witness."

American conservatives are frightened by this egalitarianism, or maybe just appalled by it. It's not traditional. But they don't want to talk about that tradition or their enthusiasm for it, though if you follow their assault on reproductive rights, women's rights, and the late 2012–early 2013 furor over renewing the Violence Against Women Act, it's not hard to see where they stand. However, they dissembled on their real interest in stopping same-sex marriage.

Those of us following the court proceedings around, for example, California's marriage-equality battle have heard a lot about how marriage is for the begetting and raising of children, and certainly reproduction requires the union of a sperm and an egg—but those unite in many ways nowadays, including in laboratories and surrogate mothers. And everyone is aware that many children are now raised by grandparents, stepparents, adoptive parents, and other people who did not beget but love them.

Many heterosexual marriages are childless; many with children break up: they are no guarantee that children will be raised in a house with two parents of two genders. The courts have scoffed at the reproduction and child-raising argument against marriage equality. And the conservatives have not mounted what seems to be their real objection: that they wish to preserve traditional marriage and more than that, traditional gender roles.

I know lovely and amazing heterosexual couples who married in the 1940s and 1950s and every decade since. Their marriages are egalitarian, full of mutuality and generosity. But even people who weren't particularly nasty were deeply unequal in the past. I also know a decent man who just passed away, age ninety-one: in his prime he took a job on the other side of the country without informing his wife that she was moving or inviting her to participate in the decision. Her life was not hers to determine. It was his.

It's time to slam the door shut on that era. And to open another door, through which we can welcome equality: between genders, among marital partners, for everyone in every cir-cumstance. Marriage equality is a threat: to inequality. It's a boon to everyone who values and benefits from equality. It's for all of us.

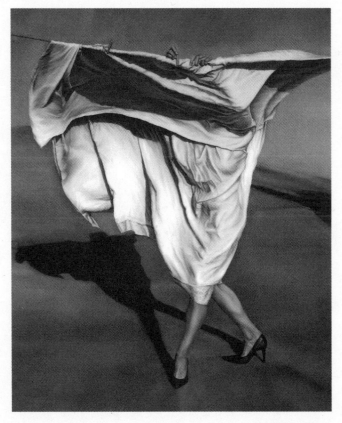

CHAPTER 5

Grandmother Spider

2014

I

A woman is hanging out the laundry. Everything and nothing happens. Of her flesh we see only several fingers and a pair of strong brown calves and feet. The white sheet hangs in front of her, but the wind blows it against her body, revealing her contours. It is the most ordinary act, this putting out clothes to dry, though she wears black high heels, as though dressed for something other than domestic work, or as if this domestic work was already a kind of dancing. Her crossed legs look as though they are executing a dance step. The sun throws her shadow and the dark shadow of the white sheet onto the ground. The shadow looks like a long-legged dark bird, another species stretching out from her feet. The sheet flies in the wind, her shadow flies, and she does all this in a landscape so bare and stark and without scale that it's as though you can see the curvature of the Earth on the horizon. It's the most ordinary and extraordinary act, the hanging out of laundry—and painting. The latter does what the wordless can do, invoking everything and saying nothing, inviting meaning in without committing to any particular one, giving you an open question rather than answers. Here, in this painting by Ana Teresa Fernandez, a woman both exists and is obliterated.

II

I think a lot about that obliteration. Or rather that obliteration keeps showing up. I have a friend whose family tree has been traced back a thousand years, but no women exist on it. She just discovered that she herself did not exist, but her brothers did. Her mother did not exist, and nor did her father's mother. Or her mother's father. There were no grandmothers. Fathers have sons and grandsons and so the lineage goes, with the name passed on; the tree branches, and the longer it goes on the more people are

missing: sisters, aunts, mothers, grandmothers, great-grandmothers, a vast population made to disappear on paper and in history. Her family is from India, but this version of lineage is familiar to those of us in the West from the Bible where long lists of
begats link fathers to sons. The crazy fourteen-generation genealogy given in the New Testament's Gospel According to Matthew
goes from Abraham to Joseph (without noting that God and not
Joseph is supposed to be the father of Jesus). The Tree of Jesse—a
sort of totem pole of Jesus's patrilineage as given in Matthew—was
represented in stained glass and other medieval art and is said to
be the ancestor of the family tree. Thus coherence—of patriarchy,
of ancestry, of narrative—is made by erasure and exclusion.

III

Eliminate your mother, then your two grandmothers, then
your four great-grandmothers. Go back more generations and
hundreds, then thousands disappear. Mothers vanish, and the
fathers and mothers of those mothers. Ever more lives disappear as if unlived until you have narrowed a forest down to a
tree, a web down to a line. This is what it takes to construct a
linear narrative of blood or influence or meaning. I used to see
it in art history all the time, when we were told that Picasso
begat Pollock and Pollock begat Warhol and so it went, as

though artists were influenced only by other artists. Decades ago, the Los Angeles artist Robert Irwin famously dumped a New York art critic on the side of the freeway after the latter refused to recognize the artistry of a young car customizer making hot rods. Irwin had been a car customizer himself, and hot-rod culture had influenced him deeply. I remember a contemporary artist who was more polite but as upset as Irwin when she was saddled with a catalogue essay that gave her a paternalistic pedigree, claiming she was straight out of Kurt Schwitters and John Heartfield. She knew she came out of hands-on work, out of weaving and all the practical acts of making, out of cumulative gestures that had fascinated her since bricklayers came to her home when she was a child. Everyone is influenced by those things that precede formal education, that come out of the blue and out of everyday life. Those excluded influences I call the grandmothers.

IV

There are other ways women have been made to disappear. There is the business of naming. In some cultures women keep their names, but in most their children take the father's name, and in the English-speaking world until very recently, married women were addressed by their husbands' names, prefaced by

Mrs. You stopped, for example, being Charlotte Brontë and became Mrs. Arthur Nicholls. Names erased a woman's genealogy and even her existence. This corresponded to English law, as Blackstone enunciated it in 1765:

> By marriage, the husband and wife are one person in law: that is, the very being or legal existence of the woman is suspended during the marriage, or at least is incorporated and consolidated into that of the husband; under whose wing, protection, and *cover*, she performs every thing; and is therefore called in our law-French a *femme-covert* . . . or under the protection and influence of her husband, her *baron*, or lord; and her condition during her marriage is called her *coverture*. For this reason, a man cannot grant anything to his wife, or enter into covenant with her: for the grant would be to suppose her separate existence.

He covered her like a sheet, like a shroud, like a screen. She had no separate existence.

V

There are so many forms of female nonexistence. Early in the war in Afghanistan, the *New York Times* Sunday magazine ran a cover story on the country. The big image at the head of the story was supposed to show a family, but I saw only a man and children, until I realized with astonishment that what I had taken for drapery or furniture was a fully veiled woman. She had disappeared from view, and whatever all the other arguments may be about veils and burkas, they make people literally disappear. Veils go a long way back. They existed in Assyria more than three thousand years ago, when there were two kinds of women, respectable wives and widows who had to wear veils, and prostitutes and slave girls who were forbidden to do so. The veil was a kind of wall of privacy, the marker of a woman for one man, a portable architecture of confinement. Less portable kinds of architecture kept women confined to houses, to the domestic sphere of housework and childrearing, and so out of public life and incapable of free circulation. In so many societies, women have been confined to the house to control their erotic energies, necessary in a patrilineal world so that fathers could know who their sons were and construct their own lineage of begats. In matrilinear societies, that sort of control is not so essential.

VI

In Argentina during the "dirty war" from 1976 to 1983, the military junta was said to "disappear" people. They disappeared dissidents, activists, left-wingers, Jews, both men and women. Those to be disappeared were, if at all possible, taken secretly, so that even the people who loved them might not know their fate. Fifteen thousand to thirty thousand Argentines were thus eradicated. People stopped talking to their neighbors and their friends, silenced by the fear that anything, anyone, might betray them. Their existence grew ever thinner as they tried to protect themselves against nonexistence. The word *disappear,* a verb, became a noun as so many thousands were transformed into the disappeared, *los desaparecidos,* but the people who loved them kept them alive. The first voices against this disappearance, the first who overcame their fear, spoke up, and became visible, were those of mothers. They were called *Las Madres de la Plaza de Mayo.* Their name came from the fact that they were the mothers of the disappeared and that they began appearing in a place that represented the very heart of the country—in front of the Casa Rosa, the presidential mansion, at the Plaza de Mayo in the capital, Buenos Aires – and having appeared, they refused to go away. Forbidden to sit, they walked. Though they would be attacked, arrested, interrogated, forced out of this most public of public places, they returned again and again to testify openly to their grief, their fury, and to mount their demand that their children and grandchildren be returned. They wore white kerchiefs embroidered with the names of their children and the date of their disappearances. Motherhood was an emotional and biological tie that the generals then in charge of the country could not portray as merely left wing or as criminal. It was a cover for a new kind of politics, as it had been for the US group Women Strike for Peace, founded in the shadow of the Cold War in 1961, when dissent was still portrayed as sinister, as communist. Motherhood and respectability became the armor, the costume, in which these women assaulted in one case the generals and in the other, a nuclear weapons program and war itself. The role was a screen behind which they had a limited kind of freedom of movement in a system in which no one was truly free.

VII

When I was young, women were raped on the campus of a great university and the authorities responded by telling all the women students not to go out alone after dark or not to be out at all. Get in the house. (For women, confinement is always waiting to envelope you.) Some pranksters put up a poster announcing another remedy, that all men be excluded from campus after dark. It was an equally logical solution, but men were shocked at being asked to disappear, to lose their freedom to move and participate, all because of the violence of one man. It is easy to name the disappearances of the Dirty War as crimes, but what do we call the millennia of disappearances of women, from the public sphere, from genealogy, from legal standing, from voice, from life? According to the project Ferite a Morte

(Wounded to Death), organized by the Italian actress Serena Dandino and her colleagues, about sixty-six thousand women are killed by men annually, worldwide, in the specific circumstances they began to call "femicide." Most of them are killed by lovers, husbands, former partners, seeking the most extreme form of containment, the ultimate form of erasure, silencing, disappearance. Such deaths often come after years or decades of being silenced and erased in the home, in daily life, by threat and violence. Some women get erased a little at a time, some all at once. Some reappear. Every woman who appears wrestles with the forces that would have her disappear. She struggles with the forces that would tell her story for her, or write her out of the story, the genealogy, the rights of man, the rule of law. The ability to tell your own story, in words or images, is already a victory, already a revolt.

VIII

You can tell so many stories about a woman hanging out the laundry—putting clothes on the line is a pleasurable task at times, a detour into the light. You can also tell many kinds of stories about the mysterious form all tangled up with a bedsheet in Ana Teresa Fernandez's painting. Hanging out the laundry might be the dreamiest of domestic chores, the one that involves air and sun and the time in which the water evaporates out of the clean clothes. It isn't done much by the privileged anymore, though whether the woman in black high heels is a housewife or a maid or a goddess at the end of the world is impossible to determine, as is the question of what it means that she's hanging out a bedsheet, though it made me think of a string of associations involving cases of obliteration—like its own laundry line. Hanging out the laundry is generally how textiles got dry until the invention of the dryer, and I still hang it out. So do Latino and Asian immigrants in San Francisco, laundry hanging out Chinatown windows and across Mission District yards, flying like so many prayer flags. What stories are told by the worn jeans, the kids' clothes, this size underwear, that striped pillowcase?

I X

This Saint Francis is wearing a white robe so all-enveloping we see only strong hands and one foot and a face in deep shadow from a hood. The light comes from the left and throws the heavy folds of what must be wool into deep shadows and ridges and his arms brought together to cradle a skull form a circle whose deep folds of cloth radiate outward. His namesake, the seventeenth-century Spanish artist Francisco de Zurbarán, painted white cloth over and over in his depictions of saints, cascading like a waterfall to hide the form of Saint Jerome, swirling in light and shadow over Saint Serapion, his arms upraised in a kind of exhausted surrender, the chains around his wrists keeping him from collapse. The fabric gesticulates, absorbs, emotes; it speaks for its shrouded figures; it replaces the sensuality of flesh with a purer but no less expressive substitute. It both hides the body and defines its space, like the bedsheet in Fernandez's painting. It's an occasion for the pure pleasure of paint, of light and shadow, and it's a source of luminousness against the older painter's dark backgrounds. Women spun and wove most of the fabric in Zurbarán's day, but they didn't paint. I saw the exhibition of Zurbarán paintings in an old Italian town with a beautiful theater whose painted walls and ceilings reminded me of a San Francisco artist, muralist Mona Caron. Though the garlands and ribbons recalled her work, few women were able to paint then, to make images in public, to define how we look at the world, to make a living, to make something we might look at five hundred years later. In Fernandez's painting, the white fabric with the expressive creases and shadows is a bedsheet. It speaks of houses, of beds, of what happens in beds and then gets washed out, of cleaning house, of women's work. This is what it's about but not what it is. The woman who is represented is obscured, but the woman who represents is not.

X

Paint in several colors was squeezed out of tubes and mixed and applied to woven fabric stretched on a wooden frame so artfully we say we see a woman hanging out a sheet rather than oil on canvas. Ana Teresa Fernandez's image on that canvas is six feet tall, five feet wide, the figure almost life-size. Though it is untitled, the series it's in has a title: *Telaraña*. Spiderweb. The spiderweb of gender and history in which the painted woman is caught; the spiderweb of her own power that she is weaving in this painting dominated by a sheet that was woven. Woven now by a machine, but before the industrial revolution by women whose spinning and weaving linked them to spiders and made spiders feminine in the old stories. In this part of the world, in the creation stories of the Hopi, Pueblo, Navajo, Choctaw, and Cherokee peoples, Spider Grandmother is the principal creator of the universe. Ancient Greek stories included an unfortunate spinning woman who was famously turned into a spider as well as the more powerful Greek fates, who spun, wove, and cut each person's lifeline, who ensured that those lives would be linear narratives that end. Spiderwebs are images of the nonlinear, of the many directions in which something might go, the many sources for it; of the grandmothers as well as the strings of begats. There's a German painting from the nineteenth century of women processing the flax from which linen is made. They wear wooden shoes, dark dresses, demure white caps, and stand at various distances from a wall, where the hanks of raw material are being wound up as thread. From each of them, a single thread extends across the room, as though they were spiders, as though it came right out of their bellies. Or as though they were tethered to the wall by the fine, slim threads that are invisible in other kinds of light. They are spinning, they are caught in the web.

To spin the web and not be caught in it, to create the world, to create your own life, to rule your fate, to name the grandmothers as well as the fathers, to draw nets and not just straight lines, to be a maker as well as a cleaner, to be able to sing and not be silenced, to take down the veil and appear: all these are the banners on the laundry line I hang out.

CHAPTER 6

Woolf's Darkness

EMBRACING THE INEXPLICABLE

2009

"*he future is dark, which is the best thing the future can be, I think*," Virginia Woolf wrote in her journal on January 18, 1915, when she was almost thirty-three years old and the First World War was beginning to turn into catastrophic slaughter on an unprecedented scale that would continue for years. Belgium was occupied, the continent was at war, many of the European nations were also invading other places around the world, the Panama Canal had just opened, the US economy was in terrible shape, twenty-nine people had just died in an Italian earthquake, Zeppelins were about to attack Great Yarmouth, launching the age of aerial bombing against civilians, and the Germans were just weeks away from using poison gas for the first time on the Western Front. Woolf, however, might have been writing about her own future rather than the world's.

She was less than six months past a bout of madness or depression that had led to a suicide attempt, and was still being tended or guarded by nurses. Until then, in fact, her madness and the war had followed a similar calendar, but Woolf recovered and the war continued its downward plunge for nearly four more bloody years. *The future is dark, which is the best thing the future can be, I think.* It's an extraordinary declaration, asserting that the unknown need not be turned into the known through false divination or the projection of grim political or ideological narratives; it's a celebration of darkness, willing — as that "*I think*" indicates—to be uncertain even about its own assertion.

Most people are afraid of the dark. Literally when it comes to children, while many adults fear, above all, the darkness that is the unknown, the unseeable, the obscure. And yet the night in which distinctions and definitions cannot be readily made is the same night in which love is made, in which things merge, change, become enchanted, aroused, impregnated, possessed, released, renewed.

As I began writing this essay, I picked up a book on wilderness survival by Laurence Gonzalez and found in it this telling sentence: "The plan, a memory of the future, tries on reality to see if it fits." His point is that when the two seem incompatible we often hang onto the plan, ignore the warnings reality offers us, and so plunge into trouble. Afraid of the darkness of the unknown, the spaces in which we see only dimly, we often choose the darkness of closed eyes, of obliviousness. Gonzalez adds, "Researchers point out that people tend to take any information as confirmation of their mental models. We are by nature optimists, if optimism means that we believe we see the world as it is. And under the influence of a plan, it's easy to see what we want to see." It's the job of writers and explorers to see more, to travel light when it comes to preconception, to go into the dark with their eyes open.

Not all of them aspire to do so or succeed. Nonfiction has crept closer to fiction in our time in ways that are not flattering to fiction, in part because too many writers cannot come to terms with the ways in which the past, like the future, is dark. There is so much we don't know, and to write truthfully about a life, your own or your mother's, or a celebrated figure's, an event, a crisis, another culture is to engage repeatedly with those patches of darkness, those nights of history, those places of unknowing. They tell us that there are limits to knowledge, that there are essential mysteries, starting with the notion that we know just what someone thought or felt in the absence of exact information.

Often enough, we don't know such things even when it comes to ourselves, let alone someone who perished in an epoch whose very textures and reflexes were unlike ours. Filling in the blanks replaces the truth that we don't entirely know with the false sense that we do. We know less when we erroneously think we know than when we recognize that we don't. Sometimes I think these pretenses at authoritative knowledge are failures of language: the language of bold assertion is simpler, less taxing, than the language of nuance and ambiguity and speculation. Woolf was unparalleled at that latter language.

What is the value of darkness, and of venturing unknowing into the unknown? Virginia Woolf is present in five of my books in this century, *Wanderlust*, my history of walking; *A Field Guide to Getting Lost*, a book about the uses of wandering and the unknown; *Inside Out*, which focused on house and home fantasies; *The Faraway Nearby*, a book about storytelling, empathy, illness, and unexpected connections; and *Hope in the Dark*, a small book exploring popular power and how change unfolds. Woolf has been a touchstone author for me, one of my pantheon, along with Jorge Luis Borges, Isak Dinesen, George Orwell, Henry David Thoreau, and a few others.

Even her name has a little wildness to it. The French call dusk the time "*entre le chien et le loup*," between the dog and the wolf, and certainly in marrying a Jew in the England of her era Virginia Stephen was choosing to go a little feral, to step a little beyond the proprieties of her class and time. While there are many Woolfs, mine has been a Virgil guiding me through the uses of wandering, getting lost, anonymity, immersion, uncertainty, and the unknown. I made that sentence of hers about darkness the epigram that drove *Hope in the Dark*, my 2004 book about politics and possibility, written to counter despair in the aftermath of the Bush administration's invasion of Iraq.

LOOKING, LOOKING AWAY, LOOKING AGAIN

I began my book with that sentence about darkness. The cultural critic and essayist Susan Sontag whose Woolf is not quite my Woolf opened her 2003 book on empathy and photography, *Regarding the Pain of Others,* with a quote from a later Woolf. She began this way: "In June 1938 Virginia Woolf published *Three Guineas*, her brave, unwelcomed reflections on the roots of war." Sontag went on to examine Woolf's refusal of the "we" in the question that launches the book: "How in your opinion are we to prevent war?"—which she answered instead with the statement, "As a woman I have no country."

Sontag then argues with Woolf about that we, about photography, about the possibility of preventing war. She argues with respect, with an awareness that historical circumstances had changed radically (including the status of women as outsiders), with the utopianism of Woolf's era that imagined an end to war altogether. She doesn't only argue with Woolf. She argues with herself, rejecting her earlier argument in her landmark book *On Photography* that we grow deadened to images of atrocity and speculating on how we must continue to look. Because the atrocities don't end and somehow we must engage with them.

Sontag ends her book with thoughts about those in the midst of the kind of war that raged in Iraq and Afghanistan. As she wrote of people in war, "'*We'* —*this ' we' is everyone who has never experienced anything like what they went through—don' t understand. We don' t get it. We truly can' t imagine what it was like. We can' t imagine how dreadful, how terrifying, war is; and how normal it becomes. Can' t understand, can' t imagine.*"

Sontag, too, calls on us to embrace the darkness, the unknown, the unknowability, not to let the torrent of images that pour down on us convince us that we understand or make us numb to suffering. She argues that knowledge can numb as well as awaken feeling. But she doesn't imagine the contradictions can be ironed out; she grants us permission to keep looking at the photographs; she grants their subjects the right to have the unknowability of their experience acknowledged. And she herself acknowledges that even if we can't completely comprehend, we might care.

Sontag doesn't address our inability to respond to entirely

unseen suffering, for even in this era of daily email solicitations about loss and atrocity and amateur as well as professional documentation of wars and crises, much remains invisible. And regimes go to great lengths to hide the bodies, the prisoners, the crimes, and the corruption: still, even now, someone may care.

The Sontag who began her public career with an essay she entitled "Against Interpretation" was herself a celebrant of the indeterminate. In opening that essay, she wrote, "The earliest experience of art must have been that it was incantatory, magical...." Later in the essay, she adds, "Today is such a time, when the project of interpretation is largely reactive, stifling. It is the revenge of the intellect upon the world. To interpret is to impoverish." And of course she then went on to a life of interpretation that, in its great moments, joined Woolf in resisting the pigeonholes, the oversimplifications and easy conclusions.

I argued with Sontag as she argues with Woolf. In fact, the first time I met her I argued with her about darkness and, to my astonishment, did not lose. If you go to her last, posthumous essay collection, *At the Same Time: Essays and Speeches*, you will find a small paragraph of my ideas and examples interpolated in her essay, like a burr in her sock. Sontag was writing her keynote speech for the Oscar Romero Award in the spring of 2003, just as the Iraq War broke out. (The award went to Ishai Menuchin, chairman of the committee of selective refusal of military service in Israel.)

Sontag had been about nine when Woolf died. I visited her when she was seventy, in her top-floor apartment in New York's Chelsea neighborhood, with a view of the backside of a gargoyle out the window and a pile of printed-out fragments of the speech on the table. I read them while drinking a dank dandelion-root tea I suspect she'd had in her cupboard for decades, the only alternative to espresso in that kitchen. She was making the case that we should resist on principle, even though it might be futile. I had just begun trying to make the case for hope in writing, and I argued that you don't know if your actions are futile; that you don't have the memory of the future; that the future is indeed dark, which is the best thing it could be; and that, in the end, we always act in the dark. The effects of your actions may unfold in ways you cannot foresee or even imagine. They may unfold long after your death. That is when the words of so many writers often resonate most.

Here we are, after all, revisiting the words of a woman who died three quarters of a century ago and yet is still alive in some sense in so many imaginations, part of the conversation, an influence with agency. In Sontag's resistance speech published at TomDispatch that spring 2003 and in *At the Same Time* a few years later, you can see a paragraph in which Sontag refers to Thoreau's posthumous influence and to the Nevada Test Site (the place where more than a thousand nuclear bombs were detonated, and where for several years, starting in 1988, I joined the great civil-disobedience actions against the nuclear arms race). The same example ended up in *Hope in the Dark*: it was about how we antinuclear activists did not exactly shut down the Nevada Test Site, our most overt goal, but inspired the people of Kazakhstan to shut down the Soviet Test Site in 1990. Totally unforeseen, totally unforeseeable.

I learned so much from the Test Site and the other places I wrote about in my book *Savage Dreams: The Landscape Wars of the American West*, about the long arc of history, about unintended consequences, delayed impacts. The Test Site as a place of great convergence and collision—and the example of authors like Sontag and Woolf—taught me to write. And then, years later, Sontag leavened her argument about acting on principle with my examples from that kitchen conversation and some details I wrote down. It was a small impact I could have never imagined, and it took place in a year when we were both invoking Virginia Woolf. The principles we both subscribed to in the books that cited her could be called Woolfian.

TWO WINTER WALKS

To me, the grounds for hope are simply that we don't know what will happen next, and that the unlikely and the unimaginable transpire quite regularly. And that the unofficial history of the world shows that dedicated individuals and popular movements can shape history and have, though how and when we might win and how long it takes is not predictable.

Despair is a form of certainty, certainty that the future will be a lot like the present or will decline from it; despair is a confident memory of the future, in Gonzalez's resonant phrase. Optimism is similarly confident about what will happen. Both are grounds for not acting. Hope can be the knowledge that we don't have that memory and that reality doesn't necessarily match our plans; hope like creative ability can come from what the Romantic poet John Keats called Negative Capability.

On a midwinter's night in 1817, a little over a century before Woolf's journal entry on darkness, the poet John Keats walked home talking with some friends and as he wrote in a celebrated letter describing that walk, "several things dove-tailed in my mind, and at once it struck me what quality went to form a Man of Achievement, especially in Literature.... I mean Negative Capability, that is, when a man is capable of being in uncertainties, mysteries, doubts, without any irritable reaching after fact and reason."

Keats walking and talking and having several things dovetail in his mind suggests the way wandering on foot can lead to the wandering of imagination and to an understanding that is creation itself, the activity that makes introspection an outdoor pursuit. In her memoir "A Sketch of the Past," Woolf wrote, "Then one day walking round Tavistock Square I made up, as I sometimes make up my books, *To the Lighthouse*; in a great, apparently involuntary, rush. One thing burst into another. Blowing bubbles out of a pipe gives the feeling of the rapid crowd of ideas and scenes which blew out of my mind, so that my lips seemed syllabling of their own accord as I walked. What blew the bubbles? Why then? I have no notion."

Some portion of Woolf's genius, it seems to me, is that having no notion, that negative capability. I once heard about a botanist in Hawaii with a knack for finding new species by getting lost in the jungle, by going beyond what he knew and how he knew, by letting experience be larger than his knowledge, by choosing reality rather than the plan. Woolf not only utilized but celebrated the unpredictable meander, on mind and foot. Her great essay "Street Haunting: A London Adventure,"from 1930, has the light breezy tone of many of her early essays, and yet voyages deep into the dark.

It takes a fictionalized or invented excursion to buy a pencil in the winter dusk of London as an excuse to explore darkness, wandering, invention, the annihilation of identity, the enormous adventure that transpires in the mind while the body travels a quotidian course. "The evening hour, too, gives us the irresponsibility which darkness and lamplight bestow," she writes. "We are no longer quite ourselves. As we step out of the house on a fine evening between four and six, we shed the self our friends know us by and become part of that vast republican army of anonymous trampers, whose society is so agreeable after the solitude of one's own room." Here she describes a form of society that doesn't enforce identity but liberates it, the society of strangers, the republic of the streets, the experience of being anonymous and free that big cities invented.

Introspection is often portrayed as an indoor, solitary thing, the monk in his cell, the writer at her desk. Woolf disagrees, saying of the home, "For there we sit surrounded by objects which enforce the memories of our own experience." She describes the objects and then states, "But when the door shuts on us, all that vanishes. The shell-like covering which our souls have excreted to house themselves, to make for themselves a shape distinct from others, is broken, and there is left of all these wrinkles and roughnesses a central pearl of perceptiveness, an enormous eye. How beautiful a street is in winter!"

The essay found its way into my history of walking, *Wanderlust*, that is also a history of wandering and of the mind in motion. The shell of home is a prison of sorts, as much as a protection, a casing of familiarity and continuity that can vanish outside. Walking the streets can be a form of social engagement, even of political action when we walk in concert, as we do in uprisings, demonstrations, and revolutions, but it can also be a means of inducing reverie, subjectivity, and imagination, a sort of duet between the prompts and interrupts of the outer world and the flow of images and desires (and fears) within. At times, thinking is an outdoor activity, and a physical one.

In these circumstances, it is often mild distraction that moves the imagination forward, not uninterrupted concentration. Thinking then works by indirection, sauntering in a roundabout way to places it cannot reach directly. In "Street Haunting," the voyages of imagination may be purely recreational, but such meandering allowed Woolf to conceive the form of *To the Lighthouse*, had furthered her creative work in a way that sitting at a desk might not. The ways creative work gets done are always unpredictable, demanding room to roam, refusing schedules and systems. They cannot be reduced to replicable formulas.

Public space, urban space, which serves at other times the purposes of the citizen, the member of society establishing contact with other members, is here the space in which to disappear from the bonds and binds of individual identity. Woolf is celebrating getting lost, not literally lost as in not knowing how to find your way, but lost as in open to the unknown, and the way that physical space can provide psychic space. She writes about daydreaming, or perhaps evening dreaming in this case, the business of imagining yourself in another place, as another person.

In "Street Haunting," she wonders about identity itself:

> Or is the true self neither this nor that, neither here nor
> there, but something so varied and wandering that it is only
> when we give the rein to its wishes and let it take its way
> unimpeded that we are indeed ourselves? Circumstances
> compel unity; for convenience' sake a man must be a whole.
> The good citizen when he opens his door in the evening
> must be banker, golfer, husband, father; not a nomad wan-
> dering the desert, a mystic staring at the sky, a debauchee in
> the slums of San Francisco, a soldier heading a revolution, a
> pariah howling with scepticism and solitude.

But he is all these others, she says, and the strictures limiting
what he can be are not her strictures.

PRINCIPLES OF UNCERTAINTY

Woolf is calling for a more introspective version of the poet
Walt Whitman's "I contain multitudes," a more diaphanous
version of the poet Arthur Rimbaud's "I is another." She is
calling for circumstances that do not compel the unity of identity that is a limitation or even repression. It's often noted that
she does this for her characters in her novels, less often that, in
her essays, she exemplifies it in the investigative, critical voice
that celebrates and expands, and demands it in her insistence

on multiplicity, on irreducibility, and maybe on mystery, if mystery is the capacity of something to keep becoming, to go beyond, to be uncircumscribable, to contain more.

Woolf's essays are often both manifestoes about and examples or investigations of this unconfined consciousness, this uncertainty principle. They are also models of a counter-criticism, for we often think the purpose of criticism is to nail things down. During my years as an art critic, I used to joke that museums love artists the way that taxidermists love deer, and something of that desire to secure, to stabilize, to render certain and definite the open-ended, nebulous, and adventurous work of artists is present in many who work in that confinement sometimes called the art world.

A similar kind of aggression against the slipperiness of the work and the ambiguities of the artist's intent and meaning often exists in literary criticism and academic scholarship, a desire to make certain what is uncertain, to know what is unknowable, to turn the flight across the sky into the roast upon the plate, to classify and contain. What escapes categorization can escape detection altogether.

There is a kind of counter-criticism that seeks to expand the work of art, by connecting it, opening up its meanings, inviting in the possibilities. A great work of criticism can liberate a work of art, to be seen fully, to remain alive, to engage in a conversation that will not ever end but will instead keep feeding the imagination. Not against interpretation, but against confinement, against the killing of the spirit. Such criticism is itself great art.

This is a kind of criticism that does not pit the critic against the text, does not seek authority. It seeks instead to travel with the work and its ideas, to invite it to blossom and invite others into a conversation that might have previously seemed impenetrable, to draw out relationships that might have been unseen and open doors that might have been locked. This is a kind of criticism that respects the essential mystery of a work of art, which is in part its beauty and its pleasure, both of which are irreducible and subjective. The worst criticism seeks to have the last word and leave the rest of us in silence; the best opens up an exchange that need never end.

LIBERATIONS

Woolf liberates the text, the imagination, the fictional character, and then demands that liberty for ourselves, most particularly for women. This gets to the crux of the Woolf that has been most exemplary for me: she is always celebrating a liberation that is not official, institutional, rational, but a matter of going beyond the familiar, the safe, the known into the broader world. Her demands for liberation for women were not merely so that they could do some of the institutional things men did (and women now do, too), but to have full freedom to roam, geographically and imaginatively.

She recognizes that this requires various practical forms of freedom and power—recognizes it in *A Room of One's Own*, too often remembered as an argument for rooms and incomes, though it demands also universities and a whole world via the wonderful, miserable tale of Judith Shakespeare, the playwright's doomed sister: "She could get no training in her craft. Could she even get her dinner in a tavern or roam the streets at midnight?" Dinner in taverns, streets at midnight, the freedom of the city are crucial elements of freedom, not to define an identity but to lose it. Perhaps the protagonist of her novel *Orlando*, who lives for centuries, slipping from one gender to another, embodies her ideal of absolute freedom to roam, in consciousness, identity, romance, and place.

The question of liberation appears another way in her talk "Professions for Women," which describes with delightful ferocity the business of killing the Angel in the House, the ideal woman who meets all others' needs and expectations and not her own.

> I did my best to kill her. My excuse, if I were to be had up in
> a court of law, would be that I acted in self-defense . . .
> Killing the Angel in the House was part of the occupation of
> a woman writer. The Angel was dead; what then remained?
> You may say that what remained was a simple and common

object—a young woman in a bedroom with an inkpot. In other words, now that she had rid herself of falsehood, that young woman had only to be herself. Ah, but what is "herself"? I mean, what is a woman? I assure you, I do not know. I do not believe that you know.

By now you've noticed that Woolf says "I don't know" quite a lot.

"Killing the Angel of the House," she says further on, "I think I solved. She died. But the second, telling the truth about my own experiences as a body, I do not think I solved. I doubt that any woman has solved it yet. The obstacles against her are still immensely powerful—and yet they are very difficult to define." This is Woolf's wonderful tone of gracious noncompliance, and to say that her truth must be bodily is itself radical to the point of being almost unimaginable before she had said it. Embodiment appears in her work much more decorously than in, say, Joyce's, but it appears—and though she looks at ways that power may be gained, it is Woolfian that in her essay "On Being Ill" she finds that even the powerlessness of illness can be liberatory for noticing what healthy people do not, for reading texts with a fresh eye, for being transformed. All Woolf's work as I know it constitutes a sort of Ovidian metamorphosis where the freedom sought is the freedom to continue becoming, exploring, wandering, going beyond. She is an escape artist.

In calling for some specific social changes, Woolf is herself a revolutionary. (And of course she had the flaws and

blind spots of her class and place and time, which she saw beyond in some ways but not in all. We also have those blind
spots later generations may or may not condemn us for.) But
her ideal is of a liberation that must also be internal, emotional, intellectual.

My own task these past twenty years or so of living by words
has been to try to find or make a language to describe the subtleties, the incalculables, the pleasures and meanings—impossible to categorize—at the heart of things. My friend Chip Ward
speaks of "the tyranny of the quantifiable," of the way what can
be measured almost always takes precedence over what cannot:
private profit over public good; speed and efficiency over en-
joyment and quality; the utilitarian over the mysteries and
meanings that are of greater use to our survival and to more
than our survival, to lives that have some purpose and value that
survive beyond us to make a civilization worth having.

The tyranny of the quantifiable is partly the failure of language and discourse to describe more complex, subtle, and
fluid phenomena, as well as the failure of those who shape
opinions and make decisions to understand and value these
slipperier things. It is difficult, sometimes even impossible, to
value what cannot be named or described, and so the task of
naming and describing is an essential one in any revolt against
the status quo of capitalism and consumerism. Ultimately the
destruction of the Earth is due in part, perhaps in large part, to

a failure of the imagination or to its eclipse by systems of accounting that can't count what matters. The revolt against this destruction is a revolt of the imagination, in favor of subtleties, of pleasures money can't buy and corporations can't command, of being producers rather than consumers of meaning, of the slow, the meandering, the digressive, the exploratory, the numinous, the uncertain.

I want to end with a passage from Woolf that my friend the painter May Stevens sent me after writing it across the text of one of her paintings, a passage that found its way into *A Field Guide to Getting Lost*. In May's paintings, Woolf's long sentences are written so that they flow like water, become an elemental force on which we are all swept along and buoyed up. In *To the Lighthouse*, Woolf wrote:

> For now she need not think about anybody. She could be herself, by herself. And that was what now she often felt the need of—to think; well, not even to think. To be silent; to be alone. All the being and the doing, expansive, glittering, vocal, evaporated; and one shrunk, with a sense of solemnity, to being oneself, a wedge-shaped core of darkness, something invisible to others. Although she continued to knit, and sat upright, it was thus that she felt herself; and this self having shed its attachments was free for the strangest adventures. When life sank down for a moment, the range of experience seemed limitless. . . . Beneath it is all dark, it is all spreading, it is unfathomably deep; but now and again

we rise to the surface and that is what you see us by. Her horizon seemed to her limitless.

Woolf gave us limitlessness, impossible to grasp, urgent to embrace, as fluid as water, as endless as desire, a compass by which to get lost.

CHAPTER 7

Cassandra
Among the Creeps

T he story of Cassandra, the woman who told the truth but was not believed, is not nearly as embedded in our culture as that of the Boy Who Cried Wolf—that is, the boy who was believed the first few times he told the same lie. Perhaps it should be. The daughter of the king of Troy, Cassandra was cursed with the gift of accurate prophecies no one heeded; her people thought she was both crazy and a liar and, in some accounts, locked her up before Agamemnon took her as a spoil of war who was casually slain along with him.

I have been thinking of Cassandra as we sail through the choppy waters of the gender wars—because credibility is such a foundational power in those wars and because women are so often accused of being categorically lacking in this department.

Not uncommonly, when a woman says something that impugns a man, particularly one at the heart of the status quo, especially if it has to do with sex, the response will question not just the facts of her assertion but her capacity to speak and her right to do so. Generations of women have been told they are delusional, confused, manipulative, malicious, conspiratorial, congenitally dishonest, often all at once.

Part of what interests me is the impulse to dismiss and how often it slides into the very incoherence or hysteria of which women are routinely accused. It would be nice if, say, Rush Limbaugh, who called Sandra Fluke a "slut" and a "prostitute" for testifying to Democrats in Congress about the need to fund birth control and who apparently completely failed to comprehend how birth control works—Limbaugh the word-salad king, the factually challenged, the eternally riled—got called hysterical once in a while.

Rachel Carson was labeled thus for her landmark work on the dangers of pesticides, *Silent Spring*. Carson had put together a book whose research was meticulously footnoted and whose argument is now considered prophetic. But the chemical companies were not happy, and being female was, so to speak, her Achilles' heel. On October 14, 1962, the *Arizona Star* reviewed her book with the headline "*Silent Spring* Makes Protest Too Hysterical." The preceding month—in an article that assured readers that DDT was entirely harmless to humans—*Time* magazine had called Carson's book "unfair, one-sided, and hysterically overemphatic." "Many scientists sympathize with Miss Carson's . . . mystical attachment to the balance of nature," the review allowed. "But they fear that her emotional and inaccurate outburst . . . may do harm." Carson *was* a scientist, incidentally.

Hysteria derives from the Greek word for "uterus," and the extreme emotional state it denotes was once thought to be due to a wandering womb; men were by definition exempt from this diagnosis that now just means being incoherent, overwrought, and maybe confused. In the late nineteenth century, it was a commonly diagnosed condition. Women diagnosed with hysteria whose agonies were put on display by Sigmund Freud's teacher Jean-Martin Charcot appear, in some cases, to have been suffering from abuse, the resultant trauma, and the inability to express its cause.

The young Freud had a succession of patients whose troubles seemed to spring from childhood sexual abuse. What they were saying was unspeakable, in a sense: even today the severest traumas in war and domestic life so violate social mores and the victim's psyche that they are excruciating to articulate.

Sexual assault, like torture, is an attack on a victim's right to bodily integrity, to self-determination and self-expression. It's annihilatory, silencing. It intends to rub out the voice and rights of the victim, who must rise up out of that annihilation to speak.

To tell a story and have it and the teller recognized and respected is still one of the best methods we have of overcoming trauma. Freud's patients, amazingly, found their way to telling what they had suffered, and at first he heard them. In 1896, he wrote, "I therefore put forward the thesis that at the bottom of every case of hysteria there are one or more occurrences of *premature sexual experience.*" Then he repudiated his findings. If he believed his patients, he wrote, "in all cases, the father, *not excluding my own,* had to be accused of being perverse."

As the feminist psychiatrist Judith Herman puts it in her book *Trauma and Recovery*: "His correspondence makes clear that he was increasingly troubled by the radical social implications of his hypothesis. . . . Faced with this dilemma, Freud stopped listening to his female patients." If they were telling the truth, he would have to challenge the whole edifice of patriarchal authority to support them. Later, she adds, "with a stubborn persistence that drove him into ever greater convolutions of theory, he insisted that women imagined and longed for the abusive sexual encounters of which they complained." It was as though a handy alibi had been constructed for all transgressive authority, all male perpetrators of crimes against females. She wanted it. She imagined it. She doesn't know what she is saying.

Silence, like Dante's hell, has its concentric circles. First come the internal inhibitions, self-doubts, repressions, confusions, and shame that make it difficult to impossible to speak, along with the fear of being punished or ostracized for doing so. Susan Brison, now chair of the philosophy department at Dartmouth, was raped in 1990 by a man, a stranger, who called her a whore and told her to shut up before choking her repeatedly, bashing her head with a stone, and leaving her for dead. Afterward she found various problems in talking about the experience: "It was one thing to have decided to speak and write about my rape, but another to find the voice with which to do it. Even after my fractured trachea had healed, I frequently had trouble speaking. I was never entirely mute, but I often had bouts of what a friend labeled 'fractured speech,' during which I stuttered and stammered, unable to string together a simple sentence without the words scattering like a broken necklace."

Surrounding this circle are the forces who attempt to silence someone who speaks up anyway, whether by humiliating or bullying or outright violence, including violence unto death. This region is now notably populated by the victims of high-school and college rapes. In many cases, these young women have been hounded and threatened for speaking up;

some have become suicidal as a result; the potential crimes go uninvestigated or unprosecuted; and many American universities appear to be graduating numerous unpunished rapists these days.

Finally, in the outermost ring, when the story has been told and the speaker has not been silenced directly, tale and teller are discredited. Given the hostility of this zone, you could call the brief era when Freud listened to his patients with an open mind a false dawn. For it's particularly when women speak up about sexual crimes that their right and capacity to speak come under attack. It seems almost reflexive at this point, and there is certainly a very clear pattern, one that has a history.

That pattern was first comprehensively challenged in the 1980s. We have at this point heard way too much about the 1960s, but the revolutionary changes of the 1980s—in toppled regimes around the world and in the bedroom, the classroom, the workplace, and the streets, and even in political organizing (with the feminist-inspired rise of consensus and other anti-hierarchical, anti-authoritarian techniques)—are mostly neglected and forgotten. It was an explosive era. The feminism of that era is often dismissed as grimly antisex because it pointed out that sex is an arena of power and that power is liable to abuse and because it described the nature of some of that abuse.

Feminists didn't just push for legislation but from the mid-1970s on defined and named whole categories of violation that had previously been unrecognized. In doing so, they announced that abuse of power was a serious problem, and that the authority of men, of bosses, husbands, fathers—and adults generally—was going to be questioned. They created a framework and support network for stories of incest and child abuse, as well as rape and domestic violence. Those stories became part of the narrative explosion in our time as so many of the formerly silent spoke up about their experiences.

Part of the messiness of that era was that no one quite knew how to listen to children, or how to question them, or in some cases how to sift through their own memories or those of adult patients in therapy. The infamous McMartin Preschool abuse trial, one of the longest and most costly in this country's history, began in 1983 when a Los Angeles area mother claimed her child was molested there. The authorities not only jumped on the situation but asked parents to ask their children leading questions and employed a therapist to interview hundreds of children with more leading questions, rewards, puppets, and other tools and techniques to help them construct wild stories about satanic abuse.

The results of the McMartin trial's chaotic interrogations are sometimes cited as evidence that children are unreliable, delusional liars, but it might be useful to remember that it was the adults who were the problem in that case. Law professor Doug Linder writes that the prosecutor gave an interview in which he "acknowledges that children began 'embellishing and embellishing' their stories of sexual abuse and said that, as prosecutors, 'we had no business being in court'" and added that potentially exculpatory evidence was withheld. Even so, the accused in that long trial and a subsequent one were not found guilty, though this is seldom remembered.

On October 11, 1991, a law professor was called to testify before the Senate Judiciary Committee. The occasion was the confirmation hearing for Clarence Thomas, nominated to the Supreme Court by George H. W. Bush; the speaker speaker was Anita Hill. When asked in a private interview and then, after that interview was leaked to the press, in Senate hearings, she recounted a list of incidents in which Thomas, then her boss, made her listen to him talk about pornography he'd watched and his sexual fantasies. He also pressured her to date him. When she declined, she said, "He would not accept my explanation as being valid," as though *no* were not itself valid.

Though she was criticized for doing nothing about his conduct at the time, it's worth remembering that feminists had only recently articulated the concept and coined the term *sexual harassment,* and that only in 1986, after the incidents she described had taken place, had the Supreme Court recognized such behavior in the workplace as a violation of the law. When she did speak up about it in 1991 she was attacked, extravagantly and furiously. Her interrogators were all men, the Republicans in particular jocular and incredulous and jeering. Senator Arlen Spector asked one witness, who on the basis of a couple of fleeting encounters testified that Hill had sexual fantasies about him, "do you think it a possibility that Professor Hill imagined or fantasized the things she has charged him with? It was the Freudian framework all over again: When she said something repellent happened, she was wishing it had, and maybe she couldn't tell the difference.

The country was in an uproar and a sort of civil war, as many women understood exactly how ordinary harassment is and how many unpleasant consequences there can be for reporting it, and many men didn't get it. In the short term, Hill was subjected to a humiliating ordeal, and Thomas won the appointment anyway. The loudest accusations came from conservative journalist David Brock, who published first an article and then a whole book smearing Hill. A decade later he repented from both his attacks on her and his alignment with the Right, writing, "[D]oing everything I could to ruin Hill's credibility, I took a scattershot approach, dumping virtually every derogatory—and often contradictory—allegation I had collected on Hill from the Thomas camp into the mix. . . . She was, in my words, 'a little bit nutty and a little bit slutty.' "

In the long term, "I Believe You, Anita" became a feminist slogan, and Hill is often credited with launching a revolution in recognition of and response to workplace sexual harassment. A month after the hearings, Congress passed the Civil Rights Act of 1991, part of which allowed sexual-harassment victims to sue their employers for damages and backpay. Harassment claims skyrocketed as people were given a way to address workplace abuses. The 1992 election was nicknamed "The Year of the Woman," and Carol Mosley Braun, still the only African American woman ever elected to the Senate, won office along with more female senators and congresswomen than ever before.

Still, even now, when a woman says something uncomfortable about male misconduct, she is routinely portrayed as delusional, a malicious conspirator, a pathological liar, a whiner who doesn't recognize it's all in fun, or all of the above. The overkill of these responses recalls Freud's deployment of the joke about the broken kettle. A man accused by his neighbor of having returned a borrowed kettle damaged replies that he had returned it undamaged, it was already damaged when he borrowed it, and he had never borrowed it anyway. When a woman accuses a man and he or his defenders protest that much, she becomes that broken kettle.

Even this year, when Dylan Farrow repeated her charges that her adoptive father, Woody Allen, had molested her, she became the most broken kettle around. A host of attackers arose. Allen published a tirade, asserting he could not have molested the child in the attic room where she said he did because he didn't like that room, proposing that his daughter had been coached and "indoctrinated" by her mother, Mia, who might have ghostwritten the accusation Dylan Farrow published, and adding that Mia had "undoubtedly" gotten the idea from a song about an attic. There was another gender divide, in which many women found the young woman credible, because they'd heard it all before, while many men seemed focused on false accusations and exaggerated the frequency of such occurrences. The ghost of the McMartin Preschool trial was raised, by people who seemed to have a false memory of the trial and its outcome.

Herman's *Trauma and Recovery,* which addresses rape, child molestation, and wartime trauma together, notes:

> Secrecy and silence are the perpetrator's first line of defense. If secrecy fails, the perpetrator attacks the credibility of his victim. If he cannot silence her absolutely, he tries to make sure that no one listens. . . . After every atrocity one can expect to hear the same predictable apologies: it never happened; the victim lies; the victim exaggerates; the victim brought it on herself; and in any case it is time to forget the past and move on. The more powerful the perpetrator, the greater is his prerogative to name and define reality, and the more completely his arguments prevail.

They don't always prevail in our time. We are still in an era of battles over who will be granted the right to speak and the right to be believed, and pressure comes from both directions. From the men's rights movement and a lot of popular misinformation comes the notion that there is an epidemic of groundless accusations of sexual assault.* The implication that women as a category are unreliable and that false rape charges are the real issue is used to silence individual women and to avoid discussing sexual violence, and to make out men as the principal victims. The framework is reminiscent of that attached to voter fraud, a crime so rare in the United States that it appears to have had no significant impact on election outcomes in a very long time. Nevertheless, claims by conservatives that such fraud is widespread have in recent years been used to disenfranchise the kinds of people—poor, non-white, students—likely to vote against them.

---

* False accusations of rape are a reality, and a relatively rare one, though the stories of those convicted falsely are terrible. A British study by the Crown Prosecution Service released in 2013 noted that there were 5,651 prosecutions for rape in the period studied versus only 35 prosecutions for false allegations of rape. And a 2000 US Department of Justice report cites these estimates for the United States: 322,230 annual rapes, resulting in 55,424 reports to police, 26,271 arrests, and 7,007 convictions—or slightly more than 2 percent of rapes counted and 12 percent of rapes reported resulted in jail sentences. Of which the number that were false is undoubtedly not colossal.

I'm not arguing here that women and children don't lie. Men, women, and children lie, but the latter two are not disproportionately prone to doing so, and men—a category that includes used-car salesmen, Baron von Münchhausen, and Richard Nixon—are not possessed of special veracity. I am arguing that we should be clear that this old framework of feminine mendacity and murky-mindedness is still routinely trotted out, and we should learn to recognize it for what it is.

A friend of mine who works in sexual-harassment training at a major university reports that when she gave a presentation at the business school on her campus, one of the older male professors asked, "Why would we start an investigation based on only one woman's report?" She has dozens of stories like this, and others about women—students, employees, professors, researchers—struggling to be believed, especially when they testify against high-status offenders.

This summer, antediluvian columnist George Will claimed that there is only a "supposed campus epidemic of rape," and that when universities or feminists or liberals "make victimhood a coveted status that confers privileges, victims proliferate." Young women replied by creating the Twitter hashtag #survivorprivilege, posting remarks such as "I didn't realize it was a privilege to live with PTSD, severe anxiety & depression" and "#ShouldIBeQuiet because when i spoke out everyone said it was a lie?" Will's column hardly even constitutes a twist on the old idea that women are naturally unreliable, that there's nothing to see in all these rape charges, and that we should just move along.

I had a tiny scale model of that experience myself earlier this year. I had posted on social media a slice of an essay I'd published a few years ago about the 1970s in California. Immediately, a stranger—a man of affluence and culture—denounced me on Facebook in response to its two paragraphs about incidents in my life back then (being hit on by grown-up hippie dudes when I was embarking on my teens). Both his fury and his baseless confidence in his ability to render judgment were remarkable; he said in part, "you are exaggerating beyond reality with no more 'proof' offered than a FOX news reporter. You 'feel' it's true so you say it's true. Well I call 'bullshit.'" I should have offered proof, as though proof were possible about a host of incidents decades ago. I am like bad people who distort facts. I am subjective but believe I am objective; I feel but confuse feeling with thinking or knowing. It's such a familiar litany and a familiar rage.

If we could recognize or even name this pattern of discrediting, we could bypass recommencing the credibility conversation every time a woman speaks. One more thing about Cassandra: in the most famous version of the myth, the disbelief with which her prophecies were met was the result of a curse placed on her by Apollo when she refused to have sex with the god. The idea that loss of credibility is tied to asserting rights over your own body was there all along. But with the real-life Cassandras among us, we can lift the curse by making up our own minds about who to believe and why.

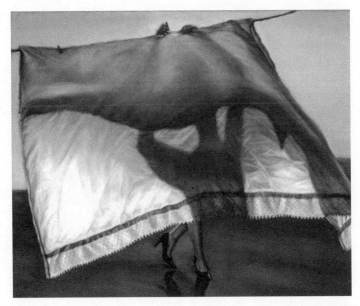

CHAPTER 8

#YesAllWomen

FEMINISTS REWRITE THE STORY

2014

I t was a key match in the World Cup of Ideas. The teams vied furiously for the ball. The all-star feminist team tried repeatedly to kick it through the goalposts marked Widespread Social Problems, while the opposing team, staffed by the mainstream media and mainstream dudes, was intent on getting it into the usual net called Isolated Event. To keep the ball out of his net, the mainstream's goalie shouted "mental illness" again and again. That "ball," of course, was the meaning of the massacre of students in Isla Vista, California, by one of their peers.

All weekend the struggle to define his acts raged. Voices in the mainstream insisted he was mentally ill, as though that settled it, as though the world were divided into two countries called Sane and Crazy that share neither border crossings nor a culture. Mental illness is, however, more often a matter of degree, not kind, and a great many people who suffer it are gentle and compassionate. And by many measures, including injustice, insatiable greed, and ecological destruction, madness, like meanness, is central to our society, not simply at its edges.

In a fascinating op-ed piece last year, T. M. Luhrmann noted that when schizophrenics hear voices in India, they're more likely to be told to clean the house, while Americans are more likely to be told to become violent. Culture matters. Or as my friend, the criminal-defense investigator who knows insanity and violence intimately, put it, "When one begins to lose touch with reality, the ill brain latches obsessively and delusionally onto whatever it's immersed in—the surrounding culture's illness."

The murderer at Isla Vista was also repeatedly called "aberrant," as if to emphasize that he was nothing like the rest of us. But other versions of such violence are all around us, most notably in the pandemic of hate toward and violence against women.

In the end, this struggle over the meaning of one man's killing spree may prove to be a watershed moment in the history of feminism, which always has been and still is in a struggle to name and define, to speak and be heard. "The battle of the story" the Center for Story-Based Strategy calls it, because you win or lose your struggle in large part through the language and narrative you use.

As media critic Jennifer Pozner put it in 2010 about another massacre by a woman-hating man:

> I am sick to death that I have to keep writing some version of this same article or blog post on loop. But I have to, because in all of these cases, gender-based violence lies at the heart of these crimes—and leaving this motivating factor uninvestigated not only deprives the public of the full, accurate picture of the events at hand, but leaves us without the analysis and context needed to understand the violence, recognize warning signs, and take steps to prevent similar massacres in the future.

The Isla Vista murderer took out men as well as women, but blowing away members of a sorority seems to have been the goal of his rampage. He evidently interpreted his lack of sexual access to women as offensive behavior by women who, he imagined in a sad mix of entitlement and self-pity, owed him fulfillment.

#YESALLWOMEN

Richard Martinez, the father of one of the young victims, spoke powerfully on national TV about gun control and the spine- lessness of the politicians who have caved to the gun lobby, as well as about the broader causes of such devastation. A public defender in Santa Barbara County, he has for decades dealt with violence against women, gun users, and mental illness, as does everyone in his field. The bloodbath was indeed about guns and toxic versions of masculinity and entitlement, and also about misery, cliché, and action-movie solutions to emo- tional problems. It was, above all, about the hatred of women.

According to one account of the feminist conversation that followed, a young woman with the online name Kaye (who has since been harassed or intimidated into withdrawing from the public conversation) decided to start tweeting with the hashtag #YesAllWomen at some point that Saturday after the massacre. By Sunday night, half a million #YesAllWomen tweets had ap- peared around the world, as though a dam had burst. And per- haps it had. The phrase described the hells and terrors women face and specifically critiqued a stock male response when women talked about their oppression: "Not all men."

It's the way some men say, "I'm not the problem" or that they shifted the conversation from actual corpses and victims as well as perpetrators to protecting the comfort level of bystander males. An exasperated woman remarked to me, "What do they want—a cookie for not hitting, raping, or threatening women?" Women are afraid of being raped and murdered all the time and sometimes that's more important to talk about than protecting male comfort levels. Or as someone named Jenny Chiu tweeted, "Sure #NotAllMen are misogynists and rapists. That's not the point. The point is that #YesAllWomen live in fear of the ones that are."

Women—and men (but mostly women)—said scathing things brilliantly.

- #YesAllWomen because I can't tweet about feminism without getting threats and perverted replies. Speaking out shouldn't scare me.
- #YesAllWomen because I've seen more men angry at the hashtag rather than angry at the things happening to women.
- #YesAllWomen because if you're too nice to them you're "leading them on" & if you're too rude you risk violence. Either way you're a bitch.

It was a shining media moment, a vast conversation across all media, including millions of participants on Facebook and Twitter—which is significant since Twitter has been a favorite means of delivering rape and death threats to outspoken women. As Astra Taylor has pointed out in her new book, *The People's Platform*, the language of free speech is used to protect hate speech, itself an attempt to deprive others of their freedom of speech, to scare them into shutting up.

Laurie Penny, one of the important feminist voices of our times, wrote:

> When news of the murders broke, when the digital world began to absorb and discuss its meaning, I had been about to email my editor to request a few days off, because the impact of some particularly horrendous rape threats had left me shaken, and I needed time to collect my thoughts. Instead of taking that time, I am writing this blog, and I am doing so in rage and in grief—not just for the victims of the Isla Vista massacre, but for what is being lost everywhere as the language and ideology of the new misogyny continues to be excused. . . . I am sick of being told to empathize with the perpetrators of violence any time I try to talk about the victims and survivors.

OUR WORDS ARE OUR WEAPONS

In 1963, Betty Friedan published a landmark book, *The Feminine Mystique*, in which she wrote, "The problem that has no name—which is simply the fact that American women are kept from growing to their full human capacities—is taking a far greater toll on the physical and mental health of our country than any known disease." In the years that followed, that problem gained several names: male chauvinism, then sexism, misogyny, inequality, and oppression. The cure was to be "women's liberation," or "women's lib," or "feminism." These words, which might seem worn out from use now, were fresh then.

Since Friedan's manifesto, feminism has proceeded in part by naming things. The term "sexual harassment," for example, was coined in the 1970s, first used in the legal system in the 1980s, given legal status by the Supreme Court in 1986, and given widespread coverage in the upheaval after Anita Hill's testimony against her former boss, Clarence Thomas, in the 1991 Senate hearings on his Supreme Court nomination. The all-male interrogation team patronized and bullied Hill, while many men in the Senate and elsewhere failed to grasp why it mattered if your boss said lecherous things and demanded sexual services. Or they just denied that such things happen.

Many women were outraged. It was, like the post–Isla Vista weekend, a watershed moment in which the conversation changed, in which those who got it pushed hard on those who didn't, opening some minds and updating some ideas. The bumper sticker "I Believe You, Anita" was widespread for a while. Sexual harassment is now considerably less common in workplaces and schools, and its victims have far more recourse, thanks in part to Hill's brave testimony and the earthquake that followed.

So many of the words with which a woman's right to exist is adjudicated are of recent coinage: "domestic violence," for example, replaced "wife-beating" as the law began to take a (mild) interest in the subject. A woman is still beaten every nine seconds in this country, but thanks to the heroic feminist campaigns of the 1970s and 1980s, she now has access to legal remedies that occasionally work, occasionally protect her, and—even more occasionally—send her abuser to jail. In 1990, the *Journal of the American Medical Association* reported, "Studies of the Surgeon General's office reveal that domestic violence is the leading cause of injury to women between the ages of fifteen and forty-four, more common than automobile accidents, muggings, and cancer deaths combined."

I go to check this fact and arrive at an Indiana Coalition Against Domestic Violence website that warns viewers their browsing history might be monitored at home and offers a domestic-violence hotline number. The site is informing women that their abusers may punish them for seeking information or naming their situation. It's like that out there.

One of the more shocking things I read recently was an essay in the *Nation* about the infamous slaying of Catherine "Kitty" Genovese in a neighborhood in Queens, New York, in 1964. The author, Peter Baker, reminds us that some of the neighbors who witnessed parts of her rape and murder from their windows likely mistook the savage assault by a stranger for a man exercising his rights over "his" woman. "Surely it matters that, at the time, violence inflicted by a man on his wife or romantic partner was widely considered a private affair. Surely it matters that, in the eyes of the law as it stood in 1964, it was impossible for a man to rape his wife."

Terms like "acquaintance rape," "date rape," and "marital rape" had yet to be invented.

TWENTY-FIRST CENTURY WORDS

Language is power. When you turn "torture" into "enhanced interrogation," or murdered children into "collateral damage," you break the power of language to convey meaning, to make us see, feel, and care. But it works both ways. You can use the power of words to bury meaning or to excavate it. If you lack words for a phenomenon, an emotion, a situation, you can't talk about it, which means that you can't come together to address it, let alone change it. Vernacular phrases—"Catch-22," "monkeywrenching," "cyberbullying," "the 99 percent and the 1 percent"—have helped us to describe but also to reshape our world. This may be particularly true of feminism, a movement focused on giving voice to the voiceless and power to the powerless.

One of the compelling new phrases of our time is "rape culture." The term came into widespread circulation in late 2012 when sexual assaults in New Delhi, India, and Steubenville, Ohio, became major news stories. As a particularly strongly worded definition puts it:

> Rape culture is an environment in which rape is prevalent and in which sexual violence against women is normalized and excused in the media and popular culture. Rape culture is perpetuated through the use of misogynistic language, the objectification of women's bodies, and the glamorization of sexual violence, thereby creating a society that disregards women's rights and safety. Rape culture affects every woman. Most women and girls limit their behavior because of the existence of rape. Most women and girls live in fear of rape. Men, in general, do not. That's how rape functions as a powerful means by which the whole female population is held in a subordinate position to the whole male population, even though many men don't rape, and many women are never victims of rape.

Sometimes I've heard "rape culture" used to describe specifically what's called "lad culture"—the jeering, leering subculture in which some young men are lodged. Other times it's used to indict the mainstream, which oozes with misogyny in its entertainment, its everyday inequalities, its legal loopholes. The term helped us stop pretending that rapes are anomalies, that they have nothing to do with the culture at large or are even antithetical to its values. If they were, a fifth of all American women (and one in seventy-one men) wouldn't be rape survivors; if they were, 19 percent of female college students wouldn't have to cope with sexual assault; if they were, the military wouldn't be stumbling through an epidemic of sexual violence. The term "rape culture" lets us begin to address the roots of the problem in the culture as a whole.

The term "sexual entitlement" was used in 2012 in reference to sexual assaults by Boston University's hockey team, though you can find earlier uses of the phrase. I first heard it in 2013 in a BBC report on a study of rape in Asia. The study concluded that in many cases the motive for rape was the idea that a man has the right to have sex with a woman regardless of her desires. In other words, his rights trump hers, or she has none. This sense of being owed sex is everywhere. Many women are told, as was I in my youth, that something we did or said or wore or just the way we looked or the fact that we were female had excited desires we were thereby contractually obliged to satisfy. We owed them. They had a right. To us.

Male fury at not having emotional and sexual needs met is far too common, as is the idea that you can rape or punish one woman to get even for what other women have done or not done. A teenager was stabbed to death for turning down a boy's invitation to go to the prom this spring; a forty-five-year-old mother of two was murdered May 14, 2014, for trying to "distance herself" from a man she was dating; the same night as the Isla Vista shootings, a California man shot at women who declined sex.

After the killings in Isla Vista, the term "sexual entitlement" was suddenly everywhere, and blogs and commentary and conversations began to address it with brilliance and fury. I think that May 2014 marks the entry of the phrase into everyday speech. It will help people identify and discredit manifestations of this phenomenon. It will help change things. Words matter.

CRIMES, SMALL AND LARGE

The twenty-two-year-old who, on May 23, 2014, murdered six of his peers and attempted to kill many more before taking his own life framed his unhappiness as due to others' failings rather than his own and vowed to punish the young women who, he believed, had rejected him. In fact, he already had done so, repeatedly, with minor acts of violence that foreshadowed his final outburst. In his long, sad autobiographical rant, he recounts that his first week in college:

> I saw two hot blonde girls waiting at the bus stop. I was dressed in one of my nice shirts, so I looked at them and smiled. They looked at me, but they didn't even deign to smile back. They just looked away as if I was a fool. In a rage, I made a U-turn, pulled up to their bus stop and splashed my Starbucks latte all over them. I felt a feeling [of] spiteful satisfaction as I saw it stain their jeans. How

dare those girls snub me in such a fashion! How dare they insult me so! I raged to myself repeatedly. They deserved the punishment I gave them. It was such a pity that my latte wasn't hot enough to burn them. Those girls deserved to be dumped in boiling water for the crime of not giving me the attention and adoration I so rightfully deserve!

Domestic violence, mansplaining, rape culture, and sexual entitlement are among the linguistic tools that redefine the world many women encounter daily and open the way to begin to change it.

The nineteenth-century geologist and survey director Clarence King and twentieth-century biologists have used the term "punctuated equilibrium" to describe a pattern of change that involves slow, quiet periods of relative stasis interrupted by turbulent intervals. The history of feminism is one of punctuated equilibriums in which our conversations about the nature of the world we live in, under the pressure of unexpected events, suddenly lurch forward. It's then that we change the story.

We are in such a crisis of opportunity now, as not one miserable, murderous young man but the whole construct in which we live is brought into question. On that Friday in Isla Vista, our equilibrium was disrupted, and like an earthquake releasing tension between tectonic plates, the realms of gender shifted a little. They shifted not because of the massacre, but because millions came together in a vast conversational network

to share experiences, revisit meanings and definitions, and arrive at new understandings. At the memorials across California, people held up candles; in this conversation people held
up ideas, words, and stories that also shone in the darkness.
Maybe this change will grow, will last, will matter, and will be a
lasting memorial to the victims.

Six years ago, when I sat down and wrote the essay "Men
Explain Things to Me," here's what surprised me: though I
began with a ridiculous example of being patronized by a man,
I ended with rapes and murders. We tend to treat violence and
the abuse of power as though they fit into airtight categories:
harassment, intimidation, threat, battery, rape, murder. But I
realize now that what I was saying is: it's a slippery slope. That's
why we need to address that slope, rather than compartmental-
izing the varieties of misogyny and dealing with each separately.
Doing so has meant fragmenting the picture, seeing the parts,
not the whole.

A man acts on the belief that you have no right to speak and
that you don't get to define what's going on. That could just
mean cutting you off at the dinner table or the conference. It
could also mean telling you to shut up, or threatening you if you
open your mouth, or beating you for speaking, or killing you to
silence you forever. He could be your husband, your father,
your boss or editor, or the stranger at some meeting or on the
train, or the guy you've never seen who's mad at someone else

but thinks "women" is a small enough category that you can stand in for "her." He's there to tell you that you have no rights.

Threats often precede acts, which is why the targets of on-line rape and death threats take them seriously, even though the sites that allow them and the law enforcement officials that generally ignore them apparently do not. Quite a lot of women are murdered after leaving a boyfriend or husband who believes he owns her and that she has no right to self-determination.

Despite this dismal subject matter, I'm impressed with the powers feminism has flexed of late. Watching Amanda Hess, Jessica Valenti, Soraya Chemaly, Laurie Penny, Amanda Marcotte, Jennifer Pozner, and other younger feminists swing into action the weekend after the Rodgers killing spree was thrilling, and the sudden explosion of #YesAllWomen tweets astonishing. The many men who spoke up thoughtfully were heartening. More and more men are actively engaged instead of just being Not All Men bystanders.

You could see once-radical ideas blooming in the mainstream media. You could see our arguments and whole new ways of framing the world gaining ground and adherents. Maybe we had all just grown unbearably weary of the defense of unregulated guns after more than forty school shootings since Sandy Hook Elementary School in December 2012, of the wages of macho fantasies of control and revenge, of the hatred of women.

If you look back to Betty Friedan's "problem that has no

name," you see a world that was profoundly different from the one we now live in, one in which women had far fewer rights and far less voice. Back then, arguing that women should be equal was a marginal position; now arguing that we should not be is marginal in this part of the world and the law is mostly on our side. The struggle has been and will be long and harsh and sometimes ugly, and the backlash against feminism remains savage, strong, and omnipresent, but it is not winning. The world has changed profoundly, it needs to change far more—and on that weekend of mourning and introspection and conversation just passed, you could see change happen.

CHAPTER 9

Pandora's Box
and the Volunteer
Police Force

2014

The history of women's rights and feminism is often told as though it were a person who should already have gotten to the last milestone or has failed to make enough progress toward it. Around the millennium lots of people seemed to be saying that feminism had failed or was over. On the other hand, there was a wonderful feminist exhibition in the 1970s entitled "Your 5,000 Years Are Up." It was a parody of all those radical cries to dictators and abusive regimes that your [fill in the blank] years are up. It was also making an important point.

Feminism is an endeavor to change something very old, widespread, and deeply rooted in many, perhaps most, cultures around the world, innumerable institutions, and most households on Earth—and in our minds, where it all begins and ends. That so much change has been made in four or five decades is amazing; that everything is not permanently, definitively, irrevocably changed is not a sign of failure. A woman goes walking down a thousand-mile road. Twenty minutes after she steps forth, they proclaim that she still has nine hundred ninety-nine miles to go and will never get anywhere.

It takes time. There are milestones, but so many people are traveling along that road at their own pace, and some come along later, and others are trying to stop everyone who's moving forward, and a few are marching backward or are confused about what direction they should go in. Even in our own lives we regress, fail, continue, try again, get lost, and sometimes make a great leap, find what we didn't know we were looking for, and yet continue to contain contradictions for generations.

The road is a neat image, easy to picture, but it misleads when it tells us that the history of change and transformation is a linear path, as though you could describe South Africa and Sweden and Pakistan and Brazil all marching along together in unison. There is another metaphor I like that expresses not progress but irrevocable change: it's Pandora's box, or, if you like, the genies (or djinnis) in bottles in the *Arabian Nights*. In the myth of Pandora, the usual emphasis is on the dangerous curiosity of the woman who opened the jar—it was really a jar, not a box the gods gave her—and thereby let all the ills out into the world.

Sometimes the emphasis is on what stayed in the jar: hope. But what's interesting to me right now is that, like the genies, or powerful spirits, in the Arabic stories, the forces Pandora lets out don't go back into the bottle. Adam and Eve eat from the Tree of Knowledge and they are never ignorant again. (Some ancient cultures thanked Eve for making us fully human and conscious.) There's no going back. You can abolish the reproductive rights women gained in 1973, with *Roe v. Wade*, when the Supreme Court legalized abortion—or rather ruled that women had a right to privacy over their own bodies that precluded the banning of abortion. But you can't so easily abolish the idea that women have certain inalienable rights.

Interestingly, to justify that right, the judges cited the Fourteenth Amendment, the constitutional amendment adopted in 1868, as part of the post–Civil War establishment of rights and freedoms for the formerly enslaved. So you can look at the antislavery movement—with powerful female participation and feminist repercussions—that eventually led to that Fourteenth Amendment, and see, more than a century later, how that amendment comes to serve women specifically. "The chickens come home to roost" is supposed to be a curse you bring on yourself, but sometimes the birds that return are gifts.

THINKING OUT OF THE BOX

What doesn't go back in the jar or the box are ideas. And revolutions are, most of all, made up of ideas. You can whittle away at reproductive rights, as conservatives have in most states of the union, but you can't convince the majority of women that they should have no right to control their own bodies. Practical changes follow upon changes of the heart and mind. Sometimes legal, political, economic, environmental changes follow upon those changes, though not always, for where power rests matters. Thus, for example, most Americans polled would like to see economic arrangements very different from those we have, and most are more willing to see radical change to address climate change than the corporations that control those decisions and the people who make them.

But in social realms, imagination wields great power. The most dramatic arena in which this has taken place is rights for gays, lesbians, and transgender people. Less than half a century ago, to be anything but rigorously heterosexual was to be treated as either criminal or mentally ill or both, and punished

severely. Not only were there no protections against such treat-
ment, there were laws mandating persecution and exclusion.

These remarkable transformations are often told as stories
of legislative policy and specific campaigns to change laws. But
behind those lies the transformation of imagination that led to
a decline in the ignorance, fear, and hatred called homophobia. American homophobia seems to be in just such a steady
decline, more a characteristic of the old than the young. That
decline was catalyzed by culture and promulgated by countless
queer people who came out of the box called the closet to be
themselves in public. As I write this, a young lesbian couple has
just been elected as joint homecoming queens at a high school
in Southern California and two gay boys were voted cutest couple in their New York high school. This may be trivial high-
school popularity stuff, but it would have been stunningly
impossible not long ago.

It's worth noting (as I have in "In Praise of the Threat" in
this book), that the very idea that marriage could extend to two
people of the same gender became far more possible because
feminists liberated marriage from the hierarchical system it had
been in and reinvented it as a relationship between equals.
Those who are threatened by marriage equality are, many
things suggest, as threatened by the idea of equality between
heterosexual couples as same-sex couples. Liberation is a con-
tagious project, speaking of birds coming home to roost.

Homophobia, like misogyny, is still terrible; just not as terrible as it was in, say, 1970. Finding ways to appreciate advances without embracing complacency is a delicate task. It involves being hopeful and motivated and keeping eyes on the prize ahead. Saying that everything is fine or that it will never get any better are ways of going nowhere or of making it impossible to go anywhere. Either approach implies that there is no road out or that, if there is, you don't need to or can't go down it. You can. We have.

We have so much further to go, but looking back at how far we've come can be encouraging. Domestic violence was mostly invisible and unpunished until a heroic effort by feminists to out it and crack down on it a few decades ago. Though it now generates a significant percentage of the calls to police, enforcement has been crummy in most places—but the ideas that a husband has the right to beat his wife and that it's a private matter are not returning anytime soon. The genies are not going back into their bottles. And this is, really, how revolution works. Revolutions are first of all of ideas.

The great anarchist thinker David Graeber recently wrote,

> What is a revolution? We used to think we knew. Revolutions were seizures of power by popular forces aiming to transform the very nature of the political, social, and economic system in the country in which the revolution took place, usually according to some visionary dream of a just society.

Nowadays, we live in an age when, if rebel armies do come sweeping into a city, or mass uprisings overthrow a dictator, it's unlikely to have any such implications; when profound social transformation does occur—as with, say, the rise of feminism—it's likely to take an entirely different form. It's not that revolutionary dreams aren't out there. But contemporary revolutionaries rarely think they can bring them into being by some modern-day equivalent of storming the Bastille. At moments like this, it generally pays to go back to the history one already knows and ask: Were revolutions ever really what we thought them to be?

Graeber argues that they were not—that they were not primarily seizures of power in a single regime, but ruptures in which new ideas and institutions were born, and the impact spread. As he puts it, "the Russian Revolution of 1917 was a world revolution ultimately responsible for the New Deal and European welfare states as much as for Soviet communism." Which means that the usual assumption that Russian revolution only led to disaster can be upended. He continues, "The last in the series was the world revolution of 1968—which, much like 1848, broke out almost everywhere, from China to Mexico, seized power nowhere, but nonetheless changed everything. This was a revolution against state bureaucracies, and for the inseparability of personal and political liberation, whose most lasting legacy will likely be the birth of modern feminism."

THE VOLUNTEER POLICE FORCE

So the cat is out of the bag, the genies are out of their bottles, Pandora's box is open. There's no going back. Still, there are so many forces trying to push us back or at least stop us. At my glummest, I sometimes think women get to choose—between being punished for being unsubjugated and the continual punishment of subjugation. If ideas don't go back in the box, there's still been a huge effort to put women back in their place. Or the place misogynists think we belong in, a place of silence and powerlessness.

More than twenty years ago, Susan Faludi published a milestone of a book called *Backlash: The Undeclared War Against American Women*. It described the double bind of women in that moment: they were getting congratulations for being fully liberated and empowered while being punished by a host of articles, reports, and books telling them that, in becoming liberated, they had become miserable; they were incomplete, missing out, losing, lonely, desperate. "This bulletin of despair is posted everywhere—at the newsstand, on the TV set, at the movies, in advertisements and doctors' offices and academic journals," wrote Faludi. "How can American women be in so much trouble at the same time that they are supposed to be so blessed?"

Faludi's answer was, in part, that, though American women had not succeeded nearly as well as so many imagined in gaining equality, they weren't suffering nearly as much as was being reported either. The articles were backlash, an attempt to push back those who were still moving forward.

Such instructions on how women are miserable and doomed haven't faded away. Here's the magazine *n+1* in late 2012, editorializing on a recent spate of backlash articles about women in the *Atlantic*:

> *Listen up ladies*, these articles say. *We're here to talk to you in a way that's limited and denigrating.* Each female author reports on a particular dilemma faced by the "modern woman," and offers her own life as a case study. . . . The problems these women describe are different, but their outlook is the same: traditional gender relations are by and large bound to endure, and genuinely progressive social change is a lost cause. Gently, like a good friend, the *Atlantic* tells women they can stop pretending to be feminists now.

A volunteer police force tries to keep women in their place or put them back in it. The online world is full of mostly anonymous rape and death threats for women who stick out— who, for instance, participate in online gaming or speak up on controversial issues, or even for the woman who recently campaigned to put women's images on British banknotes (an unusual case, in that many of those who threatened her were actually tracked down and brought to justice). As the writer Caitlin Moran tweeted: "For those who say, 'why complain—

just block?'—on a big troll day, it can be 50 violent/rape messages an hour."

Maybe there is a full-fledged war now, not of the sexes—the division is not that simple, with conservative women and progressive men on different sides—but of gender roles. It's evidence that feminism and women continue achieving advances that threaten and infuriate some people. Those rape and death threats are the blunt response; the decorous version is all those articles Faludi and *n+1* cite telling women who we are and what we may aspire to—and what we may not.

And the casual sexism is always there to rein us in, too: a *Wall Street Journal* editorial blaming fatherless children on mothers throws out the term "female careerism." *Salon* writer Amanda Marcotte notes, "Incidentally, if you Google 'female careerism,' you get a bunch of links, but if you Google 'male careerism,' Google asks if you really meant 'male careers' or even 'mahle careers.' 'Careerism'—the pathological need to have paid employment—is an affliction that only affects women, apparently."

Then there are all the tabloids patrolling the bodies and private lives of celebrity women and finding constant fault with them for being too fat, too thin, too sexy, not sexy enough, too single, not yet breeding, missing the chance to breed, having bred but failing to nurture adequately—and always assuming that each one's ambition is not to be a great actress or singer or voice for liberty or adventurer but a wife and mother. Get back in the box, famous ladies. (The fashion and women's magazines devote a lot of their space to telling you how to pursue those goals yourself, or how to appreciate your shortcomings in relation to them.)

In her great 1991 book, Faludi concludes, "And yet, for all the forces the blacklash mustered . . . women never really surrendered." Conservatives are now largely fighting rearguard actions. They are trying to reassemble a world that never really existed quite as they imagine it (and to the extent that it did, it existed at the expense of all the people—the vast majority of us—forced to disappear, into the closet, the kitchen, segregated space, invisibility and silence).

Thanks to demographics, that conservative push is not going to work—the United States is not going to be a mostly white country again—and because genies don't go back into bottles and queer people are not going back into the closet and women aren't going to surrender. It's a war, but I don't believe we're losing it, even if we won't win it anytime soon either; rather, some battles are won, some are engaged, and some women are doing really well while others suffer. And things continue to change in interesting and sometimes even auspicious ways.

WHAT DO MEN WANT?

Women are an eternal subject, which is a lot like being sub-jected, or subjugated, or a subject nation, even. There are comparatively few articles about whether men are happy or why their marriages also fail or how nice or not their bodies are, even the movie-star bodies. They are the gender that commits the great majority of crime, particularly violent crime, and they are the majority of suicides as well. American men are falling behind women in attending college, and have fallen farther in the current economic depression than women, which you'd think would make them interesting sub-jects of inquiry.

I think the future of something we may no longer call fem-inism must include a deeper inquiry into men. Feminism sought and seeks to change the whole human world; many men are on board with the project, but how it benefits men, and in what ways the status quo damages men as well, could bear far more thought. As could an inquiry into the men perpetrating most of the violence, the threats, the hatred—the riot squad of the volunteer police force—and the culture that encourages them. Or perhaps this inquiry has begun.

At the end of 2012, two rapes got enormous attention around the world: the gang-rape murder of Jhoti Singh in New Delhi and the Steubenville rape case, involving teenage assailants and victim. It was the first time I remember seeing everyday assaults on women treated more or less as lynchings and gay-bashings and other hate crimes had been: as examples of a widespread phenomenon that was intolerable and must be addressed by society, not just by individual prosecution. Rapes had always been portrayed as isolated incidents due to anomalous perpetrators (or natural uncontrollable urges or the victim's behavior), rather than a pattern whose causes are cultural.

The conversation changed. The term "rape culture" started to circulate widely. It insists that a wider culture generates individual crimes and that both must be addressed—and can be. The phrase had first been used by feminists in the 1970s, but what put it into general circulation, evidence suggests, were the Slutwalks that began in 2011 as a protest against victim-blaming.

A Toronto policeman giving a safety talk at a university told female students not to dress like sluts. Soon after, Slutwalks became an international phenomenon, of mostly young, often sexily dressed women taking back public space (rather like the Take Back the Night walks of the 1980s, but with more lipstick and less clothing). Young feminists are a thrilling phenomenon: smart, bold, funny defenders of rights and claimers of space—and changers of the conversation.

That policeman's "slut" comment was part of the emphasis

colleges have put on telling female students how to box themselves in safely—don't go here, don't do that—rather than telling
male students not to rape: this is part of rape culture. But a na-
tionwide movement organized by mostly female college students,
many of them survivors of campus sexual assault, has sprung up,
to force change in the way universities deal with such assaults. As
has a movement to address the epidemic of sexual assault in the
military that has also succeeded in forcing real policy changes
and prosecutions.

The new feminism is making the problems visible in new
ways, perhaps in ways that are only possible now that so much
has changed. A study of rape in Asia drew alarming conclusions
about its widespread nature but also introduced the term "sexual entitlement" to explain why so much of it takes place. The
report's author, Dr. Emma Fulu, said, "They believed they had
the right to have sex with the woman regardless of consent." In
other words she had no rights. Where'd they learn that?

Feminism, as writer Marie Sheer remarked in 1986, "is the
radical notion that women are people," a notion not universally accepted but spreading nonetheless. The changing conversation is encouraging, as is the growing engagement of men
in feminism. There were always male supporters. When the
first women's rights convention was held in Seneca Falls, New
York, in 1848, thirty-two of the one hundred signatories to its
Declaration of Independence—echoing manifesto were men.

Still, it was seen as a women's problem. Like racism, misogyny can never be adequately addressed by its victims alone. The men who get it also understand that feminism is not a scheme to deprive men but a campaign to liberate us all.

There's more that we need to be liberated from: maybe a system that prizes competition and ruthlessness and short-term thinking and rugged individualism, a system that serves environmental destruction and limitless consumption so well—that arrangement you can call capitalism. It embodies the worst of machismo while it destroys what's best on Earth. More men fit into it better, but it doesn't really serve any of us. You can look to movements, such as the Zapatista revolution, which has a broad ideology that includes feminist as well as environmental, economic, indigenous, and other perspectives. This may be the future of feminism that is not feminism alone. Or the present of feminism: the Zapatistas rose up in 1994 and are still going, as are myriad other projects to reimagine who we are, what we want, and how we might live.

When I attended a 2007 Zapatista *encuentro* in the Lacandon forest, focusing on women's voices and rights, at the end of 2007, women testified movingly about how their lives had changed when they had gained rights in the home and the community as part of their revolution. "We had no rights," one of them said of the era before the rebellion. Another testified, "The saddest part is that we couldn't understand our own difficulties, why we were being abused. No one had told us about our rights."

Here is that road, maybe a thousand miles long, and the woman walking down it isn't at mile one. I don't know how far she has to go, but I know she's not going backward, despite it all—and she's not walking alone. Maybe it's countless men and women and people with more interesting genders.

Here's the box Pandora held and the bottles the genies were released from; they look like prisons and coffins now. People die in this war, but the ideas cannot be erased.

Image Credits

All images by Ana Teresa Fernandez courtesy of the artist and Gallery Wendi Norris. anateresafernandez.com

1. "Untitled" (performance documentation), oil on canvas, 6"x8", from the series "Pressing Matters."
2. "Aquarius" (performance documentation at San Diego/Tijuana border), oil on canvas, 54"x82", from the series "Ablution."
3. "Untitled" (performance documentation at San Diego/Tijuana border), oil on canvas, 60"x72", from the series "Pressing Matters."

4. "Untitled" (performance documentation), oil on canvas, 70"x80", from the series "Ablution."

5. "Untitled" (performance documentation), oil on canvas, 72"x60", from the series "Teleraña."

6. "Untitled" (performance documentation), oil on canvas, 72"x60", from the series "Teleraña."

7. "Untitled" (performance documentation), oil on canvas, 53"x57", from the series "Ablution."

8. "Untitled" (performance documentation), oil on canvas, 8"x10", from the series "Teleraña."

9. "Entre"(performance documentation between Tijuana/San Diego Border Fence), oil on canvas, 30"x40".

Acknowledgments

There are so many people to thank. Marina Sitrin was a great friend and supporter and "Men Explain Things" was written at her instigation, and for, in part, her younger sister Sam Sitrin, and Sallie Shatz took me to that strange party in Colorado where it all began. Friendship with older feminists, notably Lucy Lippard, Linda Connor, Meridel Rubenstein, Ellen Manchester, Harmony Hammond, MaLin Wilson Powell, Pame Kingfisher, Carrie and Mary Dann, Pauline Esteves, and May Stevens has been valuable and reinforcing, as has that of younger feminists—Christina Gerhardt, Sunaura Taylor, Astra Taylor, Ana Teresa Fernandez, Elena Acevedo Dalcourt, and many others whose fierce intelligence about gender politics makes me hopeful about the future, as does the solidarity of the many men in my life and in the media who are now attuned to and audible on the issues.

But perhaps I should start with my mother, who subscribed to *Ms. Magazine* when it first appeared and kept up her subscription for years after. I think the magazine helped her, though she struggled for the four decades that followed with the usual conflicts between obedience and insurrection. For a child who had devoured the *Ladies' Home Journal*, *Women's Circle*, and anything else I could find to read, this new publication was a fiery addition to the diet and a potent tool to use to reconsider much of the status quo inside that house and outside. Which didn't make it easier to be a girl in the 1970s, but did make it easier to understand why.

My feminism waxed and waned, but the lack of freedom to move through the city for women hit me hard and personally at the end of my teens, when I came under constant attack in my urban environment and hardly anyone seemed to think that it was a civil rights issue or a crisis or an outrage rather than a reason why I should take taxis and martial arts classes, or take men (or weapons) with me everywhere, or take on the appearance of a man, or take myself to suburbia. I didn't do any of those things, but I did think about the issue a lot (and "The Longest War" is, for me, the third visit to that violent territory of women and public space).

Women's work, like much blue-collar work and agrarian work, is often invisible and uncredited, the work that holds the world together—maintenance work as the great feminist artist Mierle Laderman Ukeles called it in her Maintenance Art manifesto. Much culture also works that way, and though I have been the named artist on all my books and essays, good editors have been the quiet forces that make the work possible some of the time and better. Tom Engelhardt, the editor who is also my friend and collaborator, has opened the door for much of my writing in the past decade, since I sent him an unsolicited essay in 2003. TomDispatch has been a paradise of like-minded people, of a small organization with a powerful reach, of a place where my voice doesn't have to be squashed or homogenized to fit. It is telling that more than half the material in this book was written for TomDispatch, the letterbox in which I send letters to the world (and which the world seems to receive very well, thanks to the site's amazing distribution).

The essays that appear in this book are edited versions of work previously published. "The Longest War" and the other essays in this book that first appeared at TomDispatch were studded with links to sources for statistics, anecdotes, and quotes. They would have made ponderous footnotes, so those sources are not given here but can be found in the online versions.

"Men Explain Things to Me," "The Longest War," "Worlds Collide in a Luxury Suite," "Pandora's Box and the Volunteer Police Force" and "#YesAllWomen: Feminists Rewrite the Story" all appeared at TomDispatch.

"In Praise of the Threat" is the only thing that I've ever published in the *Financial Times*. It came out there on May 24, 2013, as "More Equal Than Others": http://www.ft.com/intl/cms/s/2/99659a2a-c349-11e2-9bcb-00144feab7de.html.

"Grandmother Spider" was written for the one hundredth issue of *Zyzzva Magazine*, the San Francisco—based literary journal.

And the essay on Virginia Woolf was originally a keynote lecture to the binational Nineteenth Annual Conference on Virginia Woolf in 2009 at Fordham University.

"Cassandra Among the Creeps" appeared in the October 2014 issue of *Harper's* magazine and is reprinted by kind permission of that publication

About Dispatch Books

As an editor at Pantheon Books in the 1970s and 1980s, Tom Engelhardt used to jokingly call himself publishing's "editor of last resort." His urge to rescue books and authors rejected elsewhere brought the world Eduardo Galeano's beautiful *Memory of Fire* trilogy and Art Spiegelman's Pulitzer Prize-winning *Maus*, among other notable, incendiary, and worthy works. In that spirit, he and award-winning journalist Nick Turse founded Dispatch Books, a publishing effort offering a home to authors used to operating outside the mainstream.

With an eye for well-crafted essays, illuminating long-form investigative journalism, and compelling subjects given short shrift by the big publishing houses, Engelhardt and Turse seek to provide readers with electronic and print books of conspicuous quality offering unique perspectives found nowhere else. In a world in which publishing giants take fewer and fewer risks and style regularly trumps substance, Dispatch Books aims to be the informed reader's last refuge for uncommon voices, new perspectives, and provocative critiques.

Dispatch Books' first effort, *Terminator Planet*, explored the military's increasing use of remotely piloted drones, which have turned visions of a dystopian future into an increasingly dystopian present. Now teamed with Haymarket Books, one of the leading progressive publishers in the United States, Dispatch Books exposed and analyzed the new model of US warfare with *The Changing Face of Empire* by Nick Turse and explored the untold story of how the wounded return from America's wars in *They Were Soldiers* by Ann Jones.

About Haymarket Books

Haymarket Books is a nonprofit, progressive book distributor and publisher, a project of the Center for Economic Research and Social Change. We believe that activists need to take ideas, history, and politics into the many struggles for social justice today. Learning the lessons of past victories, as well as defeats, can arm a new generation of fighters for a better world. As Karl Marx said, "The philosophers have merely interpreted the world; the point however is to change it."

We take inspiration and courage from our namesakes, the Haymarket Martyrs, who gave their lives fighting for a better world. Their 1886 struggle for the eight-hour day, which gave us May Day, the international workers' holiday, reminds workers around the world that ordinary people can organize and struggle for their own liberation. These struggles continue today across the globe—struggles against oppression, exploitation, hunger, and poverty.

It was August Spies, one of the Martyrs who was targeted for being an immigrant and an anarchist, who predicted the battles being fought to this day. "If you think that by hanging us you can stamp out the labor movement," Spies told the judge, "then hang us. Here you will tread upon a spark, but here, and there, and behind you, and in front of you, and everywhere, the flames will blaze up. It is a subterranean fire. You cannot put it out. The ground is on fire upon which you stand."

We could not succeed in our publishing efforts without the generous financial support of our readers. Many people contribute to our project through the Haymarket Sustainers program, where donors receive free books in return for their monetary support. If you would like to be a part of this program, please contact us at info@haymarketbooks.org.

© Jim Herrington

About the Author

Writer, historian, and activist Rebecca Solnit is the author of
sixteen books about environment, landscape, community, art,
politics, hope, and memory, including *Hope in the Dark: Untold
Histories, Wild Possibilities* (which began as her first TomDispatch
essay back in 2003); *The Faraway Nearby*; *A Paradise Built in Hell: The
Extraordinary Communities that Arise in Disaster*; *A Field Guide to Getting Lost*;
Wanderlust: A History of Walking; and *River of Shadows: Eadweard Muybridge
and the Technological Wild West* (for which she received a Guggen-
heim, the National Book Critics Circle Award in criticism, and
the Lannan Literary Award); and atlases of San Francisco and
New Orleans. A product of the California public education
system from kindergarten to graduate school, she is a con-
tributing editor to *Harper's* and frequent contributor to
TomDispatch.